Ⅱ   THE GEMINI ENIGMA   Ⅱ

Cracking the Code

ALSO BY JANE RIDDER-PATRICK

A Handbook of Medical Astrology
Shaping Your Future (Series of 12 titles)
Shaping Your Relationships (Series of 12 titles)

The Zodiac Code series

THE
GEMINI
ENIGMA

Cracking the Code

JANE RIDDER-PATRICK

MAINSTREAM
PUBLISHING
EDINBURGH AND LONDON

For Katze, with great affection

First published in Great Britain in 2004 by
MAINSTREAM PUBLISHING COMPANY
(EDINBURGH) LTD
7 Albany Street
Edinburgh EH1 3UG

ISBN 1 84018 527 9

A catalogue record for this book is available
from the British Library

Typeset in Allise and Van Dijck

Printed in Great Britain by
Antony Rowe Ltd., Chippenham, Wiltshire

Contents

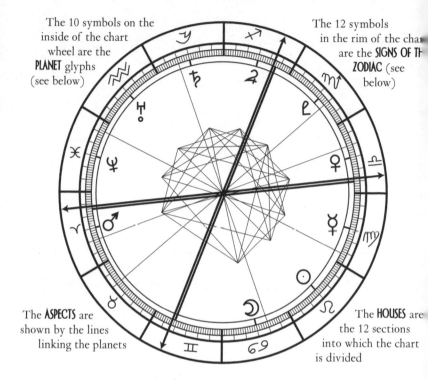

The 10 symbols on the inside of the chart wheel are the **PLANET** glyphs (see below)

The 12 symbols in the rim of the chart are the **SIGNS OF THE ZODIAC** (see below)

The **ASPECTS** are shown by the lines linking the planets

The **HOUSES** are the 12 sections into which the chart is divided

A Sample Birth Chart

Sign	Ruler	Sign	Ruler
Aries ♈	Mars ♂	Libra ♎	Venus ♀
Taurus ♉	Venus ♀	Scorpio ♏	Pluto ♇
Gemini ♊	Mercury ☿	Sagittarius ♐	Jupiter ♃
Cancer ♋	Moon ☽	Capricorn ♑	Saturn ♄
Leo ♌	Sun ☉	Aquarius ♒	Uranus ♅
Virgo ♍	Mercury ☿	Pisces ♓	Neptune ♆

ONE

The Truth of Astrology

MOST PEOPLE'S FIRST EXPERIENCE OF ASTROLOGY IS THROUGH newspapers and magazines. This is a mixed blessing for astrology's reputation – writing an astrology column to any degree of accuracy is a tough, many would say impossible, challenge. The astrologer has to try to say something meaningful about conditions that affect every single person belonging to the same sign, over a very short period of time, in a scant handful of words. The miracle is that some talented astrologers do manage to get across a tantalising whiff of the real thing and keep readers coming back for more of what most of us are hungry for – self-knowledge and reassurance about the future. The downside of the popularity of these columns is that many people think that all astrology is a branch of the entertainment industry and is limited to light-hearted fortune-telling. This is far from the truth.

What Astrology Can Offer
Serious astrology is one of the most sophisticated tools available to help us understand ourselves and the world

around us. It gives us a language and a framework to examine and describe – quite literally – *anything* under the Sun, from countries to companies, from money markets to medical matters. Its most common application, however, is in helping people to understand themselves better using their own unique birth charts. Astrology has two main functions. One is to describe the traits and tendencies of whatever it is that is being examined, whether this is a state, a software company or someone's psyche. The other is to give an astonishingly accurate timetable for important changes within that entity. In the chapters that follow, we'll be using astrology to investigate the psychology of the innermost part of your personality, taking a look at what drives, inspires and motivates you.

Astrology uses an ancient system of symbols to describe profound truths about the nature of life on earth, truths that cannot be weighed and measured, but ones we recognise nevertheless, and that touch and move us at a deep level. By linking mythology and mathematics, astrology bridges the gap between our inner lives and our outer experiences, between mind and matter, between poetry and science.

Fate and Free Will

Some people think that astrology is all about foretelling the future, the implication being that everything is predestined and that we have no say in how our lives take shape. None of that is true. We are far from being helpless victims of fate. Everything that happens to us at any given time is the result of past choices. These choices may have been our own, or made by other people. They could even have been made long ago before we, or even our grandparents, were born. It is not always possible to prevent processes that were set in motion in the past from coming to their logical conclusions as events that we then have to deal with. We are, however, all free to decide how to react to whatever is presented to us at every moment of our lives.

Your destiny is linked directly with your personality because the choices you make, consciously or unconsciously, depend largely on your own natural inclinations. It is these inclinations that psychological astrology describes. You can live out every single part of your chart in a constructive or a less constructive way. For instance, if you have Aries strong in your chart, action and initiative will play a major role in your life. It is your choice whether you express yourself aggressively or assertively, heroically or selfishly, and also whether you are the doer or the done-to. Making the right choices is important because every decision has consequences – and what you give out, sooner or later, you get back. If you don't know and understand yourself, you are 'fated' to act according to instinct and how your life experiences have conditioned you. By revealing how you are wired up temperamentally, astrology can highlight alternatives to blind knee-jerk reactions, which often make existing problems worse. This self-knowledge can allow you to make more informed free-will choices, and so help you create a better and more successful future for yourself.

Astrology and Prediction

Astrology cannot predict specific events based on your birth chart. That kind of prediction belongs to clairvoyance and divination. These specialities, when practised by gifted and responsible individuals, can give penetrating insights into events that are likely to happen in the future if matters proceed along their present course.

The real benefit of seeing into the future is that if we don't like what could happen if we carry on the way we're going, we can take steps either to prevent it or to lessen its impact. Rarely is the future chiselled out in stone. There are many possible futures. What you feed with your attention grows. Using your birth chart, a competent astrologer can map out, for years in advance, major turning points, showing which areas of your life will be affected at these times and the kind of change that will be taking place. This information gives answers to the questions that most clients ask in one way or another: 'Why me, why this and why now?' If you accept responsibility for facing what needs to be done at the appropriate time, and doing it, you can change the course of your life for the better.

Astrology and the Soul

What is sometimes called the soul and its purpose is a mystery much more profound than astrology. Most of us have experienced 'chance' meetings and apparent 'tragedies' which have affected the direction of our entire lives. There is an intelligence at work that is infinitely wiser and more powerful than the will or wishes of our small egocentric personalities. This force, whatever name we give it – Universal Wisdom, the Inner Guide, the Self, a guardian angel – steers us into exactly the right conditions for our souls' growth. Astrology can pinpoint the turning points in the course of your destiny and describe the equipment that you have at your disposal for serving, or resisting, the soul's purpose. That equipment is your personality.

Who Are You?

You are no doubt aware of your many good qualities as well as your rather more resistible ones that you might prefer to keep firmly under wraps. Maybe you have wondered why it is that one part of your personality seems to want to do one thing while another part is stubbornly intent on doing the exact opposite. Have you ever wished that you could crack the code that holds the secrets of what makes you – and significant others – behave in the complex way you do? The good news is that you can, with the help of your astrological birth chart, sometimes known as your horoscope.

Just as surely as your DNA identifies you and distinguishes you from everyone else, as well as encoding your peculiarities and potential, your birth chart reveals the unique 'DNA fingerprinting' of your personality. This may seem a staggering claim, but it is one that those who have experienced serious astrology will endorse, so let's take a closer look at what a birth chart is.

Your Birth Chart

Your birth chart is a simplified diagram of the positions of the planets, as seen from the place of your birth, at the moment you took your first independent breath. Critics have said that astrology is obviously nonsense because birth charts are drawn up as if the Sun and all the planets moved round the Earth.

We know in our minds that the Earth moves round the Sun, but that doesn't stop us seeing the Sun rise in the east in the morning and move across the sky to set in the west in the evening. This is an optical illusion. In the same way, we know (or at least most of us know) that we are not really the centre of the universe, but that doesn't stop us experiencing ourselves as being at the focal point of our own personal worlds. It is impossible to live life in any other way. It is the strength, not weakness, of astrology that it describes from your own unique viewpoint how you, as an individual, experience life.

Erecting Your Chart

To draw up a full birth chart you need three pieces of information – the date, time and place of your birth. With your birth date alone you can find the positions of all the planets (except sometimes the Moon) to a good enough degree of accuracy to reveal a great deal of important information about you. If you have the time and place of birth, too, an astrologer can calculate your Ascendant or Rising Sign and the houses of your chart – see below. The Ascendant is a bit like the front door of your personality and describes your general outlook on life. (If you know your Ascendant sign, you might like to read more about its characteristics in the book on that sign in this series.)

The diagram on page 6 shows what a birth chart looks like. Most people find it pretty daunting at first sight but it actually breaks down into only four basic units – the planets, the signs, the aspects and the houses.

The Planets

Below is a simple list of what the planets represent.

PLANET	REPRESENTS YOUR URGE TO
☉ The Sun	express your identity
☽ The Moon	feel nurtured and safe
☿ Mercury	make connections
♀ Venus	attract what you love
♂ Mars	assert your will
♃ Jupiter	find meaning in life
♄ Saturn	achieve your ambitions
♅ Uranus	challenge tradition
♆ Neptune	serve an ideal
♇ Pluto	eliminate, transform and survive

The planets represent the main psychological drives that every single one of us has. The exact way in which we express these drives is not fixed from birth but develops and evolves throughout our lives, both consciously and unconsciously. In this book we will be examining in detail four of these planets – your Sun, Moon, Mercury and Venus. These are the bodies that are right at the heart of our solar system. They correspond, in psychological astrology, to the core of your personality and represent how you express yourself, what motivates you emotionally, how you use your mind and what brings you pleasure.

The Signs

The signs your planets are in show how you tend to express your inner drives. For example, if your Mars is in the action sign of Aries, you will assert yourself pretty directly, pulling no punches. If your Venus is in secretive Scorpio, you will attract, and also be attracted to, emotionally intense relationships. There is a summary of all of the signs on p. 128.

The Aspects

Aspects are important relationships between planets and whether your inner characteristics clash with or complement each other depends largely on whether or not they are in aspect and whether that aspect is an easy or a challenging one. In Chapter Six we'll be looking at some challenging aspects to the Sun.

The Houses

Your birth chart is divided into 12 slices, called houses, each of which is associated with a particular area of life, such as friendships, travel or home life. If, for example, you have your Uranus in the house of career, you are almost certainly a bit of a maverick at work. If you have your Neptune in the house of partnership, you are likely to idealise your husband, wife or business partner.

The Nature of Time

Your birth chart records a moment in time and space, like a still from a movie – the movie being the apparent movement of the planets round the earth. We all know that time is something that can be measured in precise units, which are always the same, like seconds, months and centuries. But if you stop to reflect for a moment, you'll also recognise that time doesn't always feel the same. Twenty minutes waiting for a bus on a cold, rainy day can seem like a miserable eternity, while the same amount of time spent with someone you love can pass in a flash. As Einstein would say – that's relativity.

There are times in history when something significant seems to be in the air, but even when nothing momentous is happening the quality of time shifts into different 'moods' from moment to moment. Your birth chart is impregnated with the qualities of the time when you were born. For example, people who were born in the mid-to-late 1960s, when society was undergoing major disruptive changes, carry those powerful energies within them and their personalities reflect, in many ways, the turmoil of those troubled and exciting times. Now, as adults, the choices that those individuals make, based on their own inner conflicts and compulsions, will help shape the future of society for better or worse. And so it goes on through the generations.

Seed Meets Soil

There is no such thing as a good or bad chart, nor is any one sign better or worse than another. There are simply 12 different, but equally important, life focuses. It's useful to keep in mind the fact that the chart of each one of us is made up of all the signs of the zodiac. This means that we'll act out, or experience, *every* sign somewhere in our lives. It is true, however, that some individual charts are more challenging than others; but the greater the challenge, the greater the potential for achievement and self-understanding.

In gardening terms, your chart is a bit like the picture on a seed packet. It shows what you could become. If the seeds are of poppies, there's no way you'll get petunias, but external conditions will affect how they grow. With healthy soil, a friendly climate and green-fingered gardeners, the plants have an excellent chance of flourishing. With poor soil, a harsh climate or constant neglect, the seeds will be forced to struggle. This is not always a disadvantage. They can become hardy and adapt, finding new and creative ways of evolving and thriving under more extreme conditions than the plant that was well cared for. It's the same with your chart. The environment you were raised in may have been friendly or hostile to your nature and it will have done much to shape your life until now. Using the insights of astrology to affirm who you are, you can, as an adult, provide your own ideal conditions, become your own best gardener and live out more fully – and successfully – your own highest potential.

TWO

The Symbolism of Gemini

WE CAN LEARN A GREAT DEAL ABOUT GEMINI BY LOOKING AT THE symbols, myths and legends associated with it. These are time-honoured ways of describing psychological truths; they carry more information than plain facts alone and hint at the deeper meanings and significance of the sign.

It's easy to see the Gemini glyph of two vertical lines with cross bars at the top and bottom as the Roman numeral for two. This points to the dual nature of the sign; the lightning-fast changeability of Geminis often gives the impression of there being two people in one. It hints too at the duality of life on earth, where everything is split into pairs of opposites, like man and woman, good and evil, up and down, right and left. Geminis love moving between two of these associated, but as yet separated, areas of life, and linking them up. The glyph can also represent a doorway between two rooms. Geminis often seem to hover on thresholds, coming in and going out at the same time, without committing themselves to any one fixed position.

The glyph is said to show the two great pillars of King Solomon's Temple. The white pillar, Jachin, was associated with the Sun and day, and Boaz, the black pillar, represented the Moon and night. In Freemasonry, these pillars have globes on top with a hand coming out from each clasping the other in a masonic handshake. Inscribed above, in Latin, are the words which mean 'Reason and Experience Joined'. There could hardly be a better motto for Gemini.

Gemini the Twins

Gemini is the Latin word for twins. In ancient times, twins were seen as guardians of all doorways and statues of twins were found at the gates of Babylonian, Egyptian and Assyrian temples and houses. They were also thought to bring good fortune to travellers and sailors, so ships often had twins as a figurehead for luck. An ancient esoteric symbol for Gemini is two monkeys. One is a chattering no-brain, imitating everything it sees without the slightest understanding of what it is doing or why; the other is the great ape whose consciousness has evolved and has therefore become divine. Gemini, the choice of role model is yours . . .

Ruled by Mercury

Each sign is associated with a planet, known as its ruler. Mercury, Gemini's ruler, is the smallest and fastest planet in the solar system and the one closest to the Sun. This makes it difficult to see, and it can certainly be hard to spot what Geminis are up to in the blinding light and speed of their logic.

The Roman god Mercury was known as Hermes in Greek mythology. Hermes has two faces, just like Gemini. He was the god of thieves, liars and merchants, as well as being the patron of magicians and the protector of roads and travelling. He was the trusted messenger of all of the gods, not just one or two, yet was also an ingenious and witty trickster who would sometimes, quite deliberately, lead people astray. Curiously, this usually brought them – eventually and by way of many apt adventures – to exactly where they needed to be, a place that often couldn't have been arrived at otherwise. As the only god who could move freely between the three realms of heaven, earth and the underworld, acting as go-between, Hermes reflects the complex nature of Geminis who are at home in the superficialities of worldly chatter, fascinated by the depths of the psyche, and are often attracted to the spiritual realm, yet seem unable, or unwilling, to settle in any of them.

In his mature form, Hermes is the guide and escort of souls and the arranger of synchronicities and coincidences – things happening at just the right time for no apparent reason. He is the god of kairos, the potent time when transformation can take place. The Greek word *kairos* refers to the moment in weaving when the two sets of warp threads are held apart and the weft thread, carried by the shuttle, can be passed through. This is a moment when something new – in the fabric of life itself – is actually being created. It is your task, as a Gemini, to act as a shuttle, an agent of creative connections.

Gemini in Myth and Legend

The twins most often associated with Gemini are Castor and Pollux of Greek mythology. Their father was Zeus, the chief god, and their mother, Leda, a mortal woman. Castor was human and Pollux was divine and they were inseparable until Castor was killed in battle and, being mortal, went to the underworld. Pollux was heartbroken and begged Zeus to let him die too. A deal was done (Geminis are good at deals) allowing the twins to stay together. They had to alternate between each other's territory, spending one day up in heaven and the next in the underworld. This corresponds to the split in the Gemini personality – one moment the sunny and carefree divine child, the next down in the depths of despair at the limitations of being a mere mortal. Another version of the agreement was that one twin was in heaven and the other down below but they could swap places every day and, on the way up or down, spend some time together enjoying each other's company and catching up. There's nostalgia in Gemini, an ache for a loss of completeness, and a pain at being split and not able to settle down anywhere for long. This yearning for union goes hand in hand with a resistance to it, for to commit to one thing means the loss of countless opportunities for experiencing something else.

The life of most Geminis is, at some stage, touched by a challenge or crisis concerning separation, forced or chosen, from someone or something that they love and having to come to terms with the hard and bitter truth that you cannot have your cake and eat it too. The challenge then is to find a compromise and to be willing to pay the price – which, as it was for Castor and Pollux, is the acceptance of limits – so that you can have the best of both worlds, but not all at once.

The Season of Gemini

Nature is in a transition period when the Sun is in Gemini. In the northern hemisphere, where astrology developed, the freshness of spring is giving way to the maturity of summer, spring blossoms are fading but summer flowers have not yet reached their prime. Young animals are beginning to detach from their mothers to explore the world around them. Traditionally, in the academic year, it is a time for intense study as students prepare for their end of the year examinations. For most Geminis, learning is a lifelong affair.

THREE

The Heart of the Sun

THE GLYPH FOR THE SUN IS A PERFECT CIRCLE WITH A DOT in the centre and symbolises our dual nature – earthly and eternal. The circle stands for the boundary of the personality, which distinguishes and separates each individual from every other individual, for it is our differences from other people that make us unique, not our similarities. The dot in the centre indicates the mysterious 'divine spark' within us and the potential for becoming conscious of who we truly are, where we have come from and what we may become.

The Meaning of the Sun
Each of your planets represents a different strand of your personality. The Sun is often reckoned to be the most important factor of your whole birth chart. It describes your sense of identity, and the sign that the Sun was in when you were born, your Sun sign, along with its house position and any aspects to other planets, shows how you express and develop that identity.

Your Role in Life

Each of the signs is associated with certain roles that can be played in an infinite number of ways. Take one of the roles of Aries, which is the warrior. A warrior can cover anything from Attila the Hun, who devastated vast stretches of Europe with his deliberate violence, to an eco-warrior, battling to save the environment. The role, warrior, is the same; the motivation and actions are totally different. You can live out every part of your personality in four main ways – as creator, destroyer, onlooker or victim. How you act depends on who you choose to be from the endless variations possible from the symbolism of each of your planets, but most particularly your Sun. And you do have a choice; not all Geminis are irresponsible space cadets nor is every Scorpio a sex-crazed sadist. This book aims to paint a picture of what some of your choices might be and show what choices, conscious or unconscious, some well-known people of your sign have made.

Your upbringing will have helped shape what you believe about yourself and out of those beliefs comes, automatically, behaviour to match. For example, if you believe you are a victim, you will behave like one and the world will happily oblige by victimising you. If you see yourself as a carer, life will present you with plenty to care for – and often to care about, too. If you identify yourself as an adventurer, you'll spot opportunities at every corner. If you're a winner, then you'll tend to succeed. Shift the way that you see yourself and your whole world shifts, too.

Your Vocation

Your Sun describes your major life focus. This is not always a career. As the poet Milton said: 'They also serve who only stand and wait.' It is impossible to tell from your Sun sign exactly what your calling is – there are people of all signs occupied in practically every area of life. What is important is not so much *what* you do, but the way that you do it and it is this – how you express yourself – that your Sun describes. If you spend most of your time working at an occupation or living in a situation where you can't give expression to the qualities of your Sun, or which forces you to go against the grain of your Sun's natural inclinations, then you're likely to live a life of quiet, or possibly even noisy, desperation.

On Whose Authority

Your personality, which your birth chart maps, is like a sensitive instrument that will resonate only to certain frequencies – those that are similar to its own. Your Sun shows the kind of authority that will strike a chord with you, either positively or negatively, because it is in harmony with yours. It can show how you relate to people in authority, especially your father. (It is the Moon that usually shows the relationship with your mother and home.) In adult life it can throw light onto the types of bosses you are likely to come across, and also how you could react to them. It is a major part of the maturing process to take responsibility for expressing your own authority wisely. When you do so, many of your problems with external authorities diminish or even disappear.

In a woman's chart the Sun can also describe the kind of husband she chooses. This is partly because, traditionally, a husband had legal authority over his wife. It is also because, especially in the early years of a marriage, many women choose to pour their energies into homemaking and supporting their husbands' work in the world, rather than their own, and so his career becomes her career. As a

Gemini, you may find that your father, boss or husband shows either the positive or negative traits of Gemini or, as is usually the case, a mixture of both – cultured, charming and fun or glib, irresponsible and emotionally unavailable.

Born on the Cusp

If you were born near the beginning or end of Gemini, you may know that your birthday falls on the cusp, or meeting point, of two signs. The Sun, however, can only be in one sign or the other. You can find out for sure which sign your Sun is in by checking the tables on pp. 97–8.

FOUR

The Drama of Being a Gemini

EACH SIGN IS ASSOCIATED WITH A CLUSTER OF ROLES THAT HAVE THEIR OWN core drama or storyline. Being born is a bit like arriving in the middle of an ongoing play and slipping into a certain part. How we play our characters is powerfully shaped in early life by having to respond to the input of the other actors around us – the people that make up our families and communities. As the play of our lives unfolds, we usually become aware that there are themes which tend to repeat themselves. We may ask ourselves questions like 'Why do I always end up with all the work / caught up in fights / with partners who mistreat me / in dead-end jobs / successful but unhappy . . .?' or whatever. Interestingly, I've found that people are less likely to question the wonderful things that happen to them again and again.

The good news is that once we recognise the way we have been playing our roles, we can then use our free-will choice to do some creative re-scripting, using the same character in more constructive scenarios. Even better news is that if we change, the other people in our dramas have got to make some alterations, too. If you refuse to respond to the same old cues in the customary ways, they are going to have to get creative too.

A core role of Gemini is the go-between or intermediary. A go-between operates in the no-man's-land between two people, situations or pieces of information which are separate from each other and may appear to be totally unconnected or even have conflicting agendas. Their challenging, and sometimes tricky, mission is to bridge the gap and link the two together. To do this, the intermediary needs enough knowledge of both to be able, swiftly, to spot parallels and shared interests. By identifying strands of similarity and pulling them together, a common ground can be established where a dialogue can take place. For maximum effectiveness, the go-between has to be able to speak and understand the language of both parties and needs too to be seen as fair and impartial, valuing the interests of both equally, otherwise he or she could appear to be taking sides. This is a task that requires great skill, and it is one that most born under the sign of the twins have down to a fine art. Geminis can associate easily with a range of widely differing people and give all the impression that they have their full and undivided interest and attention, which they genuinely do have – for the duration of the contact anyway. A smooth-talking tongue and creative powers of persuasion come in handy too; through the ingenious use of language and suggestion, a good intermediary is usually able to leave everyone feeling that he or she is getting an excellent bargain. Once the link-up has been accomplished and the connection or deal successfully secured, the job is over and done with. What happens from then on is of little concern and the consequences are someone else's affair. For Gemini, it's the passing-on of the baton that counts, not the follow-through.

Another major Gemini role is the reporter. Here the task is to be an onlooker and skilled observer, noticing changes, great and small, in the world around and bringing this information to the attention of others, as vividly as possible. Once the news is delivered, it's time to move on, hot on the scent of fresher novelties. Other roles are the interpreter, translator, agent, broker, trend-spotter, salesperson, student and messenger. All of these involve gathering up bits and pieces of information and then passing them on to others, either more or less unchanged or with a deft spin that makes them more interesting or advantageous to either sender or receiver or . . . both.

How you choose to see your role will determine your behaviour. The following chapter describes some typical Gemini behaviour. Remember, though, that there is no such thing as a person who is all Gemini and nothing but Gemini. You are much more complicated than that and other parts of your chart will modify, or may even seem to contradict, the single, but central, strand of your personality which is your Sun sign. These other sides of your nature will add colour and contrast and may restrict or reinforce your basic Gemini identity. They won't, however, cancel out the challenges you face as a Gemini.

FIVE

The Gemini Temperament

WITH YOUR IRREPRESSIBLE CURIOSITY AND BEACHCOMBING BRAIN, you are on a never-ending wonder quest from cradle to curtain. Your aim is to notice, to know and to interact as fully as possible with the world around you, dipping into and sampling a little of all that comes your way. Like a child let loose in a toy shop, you've no intention of allowing a single, solitary plaything to go unexamined, and you may have a child's attention span to match. When something new appears on the horizon, your scanning eyes are sure to spot it and you're liable to drop or discard what was previously so fascinating. Nothing is too large, small or obscure to investigate if it catches your interest. The word *interest* comes from the Latin meaning 'to be among or between', and that's exactly where you want to be – right in the middle of whatever is current. Happiness is a cup that's full and running over with new experiences and sensations just waiting to be sipped, tasted and savoured. For you, variety is not the spice but the very essence of life itself.

Just Passing Through

Although you are perfectly capable of serious concentration if you set your mind to it, you usually prefer to stay an enthusiastic amateur, with a wide range of interests, rather than become an in-depth expert in only a few. Just as butterflies flit from flower to flower, sipping nectar then moving on, you tend to brush lightly against life's experiences, window-shopping and browsing, but rarely staying long. The only stability you'd vote for is constant, stimulating change; predictability and boredom crush you to the core. With one hand on the doorknob and a foot over the threshold, ready to take off, ideally you'd like to be in two places at once. The Gemini Italian saint Padre Pio apparently achieved this blessed state of bilocation. There are reports of him being seen by two sets of reliable witnesses in two different places at the very same time. The past calls, yet the future beckons. If you're trapped, with all escape routes blocked, you'll tap, fidget and squirm until you're let off the hook. Driven on by an appetite for novelty, your attention quickly pounces on fresh enticements. These take discipline to resist, so any Gemini who turns up regularly for appointments exactly on time deserves a standing ovation. Practically nobody can pack more into a minute than the average Gemini. With your high-voltage energy, you can give the impression of being plugged into the mains, but missing an off switch. You seem to have more arms and legs than anyone else, not to mention mouths and tongues, and all of them active at once. You are perfectly capable of cooking a meal, watching television, checking your email, changing the baby and having a riveting conversation with a new-found friend simultaneously and – usually – effortlessly as well.

Trend-Spotting

You've a sense of what's in the air and can quickly spot up-and-coming trends in your own fields of interest. You thrive on having some connection to freshly brewing news. As you may be keen on culture, this can mean visits to the latest exhibition or the coolest new restaurant, club, film or show. But it can just as easily be keeping abreast of happenings around your own village green. Once you've made a discovery, you can't wait to pass it on. It's as instinctive as breathing – what you take in, you want to give out and share with at least one other person. You're a walking, talking information service. There is the occasional Gemini fluffhead with verbal incontinence, where trivia goes straight in the ears and eyes and out through the mouth, without the usual intermediate stage of brain engagement, but most Geminis are skilled communicators, gifted at picking out the plums which are worth passing on.

Wizards with Words

Your way with words can be downright mesmerising; you can weave spells and enchantments with simple sentences. Words are your weapons and your magic wands. With a gift for reasoning, you can spot loopholes in logic but you are also expert at playing mental loop-the-loop, using your lightning-quick responses to prove anything at all that you want to prove. You're even capable of making up, on the spot, some convoluted logic, then talking yourself into believing it too.

Fencing with a mind as clever as your own is one of life's great pleasures. Mischief appeals, and you often enjoy making great sweeping statements just to stir up controversy. You'll then run rings round your opponents with your ability to draw neat parallels, note discrepancies and elasticate the facts. Spin doctors could be distilled from pure essence of Gemini. Alastair Campbell, Tony Blair's erstwhile Press Secretary is a Gemini and Blair himself has a Gemini Ascendant. If you are feeling bored or trapped, you can execute a deft U-turn and change the subject, even in the middle of a sentence – and still make what you are saying appear perfectly plausible.

Gemini, like all of the air signs, is essentially ethical, which may seem a bit of a paradox, given your love of bendy logic. You'd rarely tell a big, brazen, barefaced lie, unless you just fancied an experiment to see what would happen. (Little polite white lies don't count. These, to you, are simply good manners.) With your command of language, there's no need to resort to such crudities. A pregnant pause, a raised eyebrow or a knowing look, rearranging or missing out a word here and there – like 'not' – can achieve a much more pleasing effect with the minimum of comeback.

As you change your mind frequently, you can seem inconsistent but as Gemini writer Walt Whitman said, 'Do I contradict myself? Very well, I contradict myself. I am large. I contain multitudes.' Sometimes these about-turns can make you appear two-faced. You can praise something one moment then condemn it the next, and often forget you have done so, but this is simply the result of living for the moment – and one moment's meat can be another moment's poison.

You seem to be able to find exactly the right phrases to fit any situation and you do love to talk. You can be witty, apt and to the point, with a clever answer for everything and a distinct preference for having the last word. When asked by a rather disapproving interviewer if she had had *anything* on when photographed for a nude calendar, Marilyn Monroe retorted immediately, 'Yes, of course – I had the radio on.' Your verbal skills and gift for mimicry could make you an excellent linguist, as you seem to assimilate words and accents with the air you breathe. A Gemini friend of mine speaks four languages fluently – one of them picked up by the age of four by hiding under her parents' dining table when foreign guests came to call.

Classified Information

You are fascinated by the interrelatedness of people and things and as you forage for new sensations and glean slivers of information, your brain is busy spotting differences and similarities, processing and classifying your experiences and building up your database for future retrieval. You like mental maps and models which help you analyse how everything works and connects together, and most especially, what makes human beings tick. This inner scaffolding, whether it's astrology, psychology or hardcore science, provides an ingenious way of ordering all the impressions that are constantly impinging on you. When some new fact comes your way, you can run it past your mental check-in desk to see where it belongs and file it away neatly like a squirrel storing up nuts for the winter. Your ability to observe, name, classify and link is one of your finest assets, but your mental cleverness can also sometimes seduce you into the illusion that the world, and all its knowledge, is an affair that can be managed by the mind alone. It's easy to forget that the map is not the territory and the description is not the experience. You can grasp in the twinkling of a brain cell the logical relationships between people or principles but may miss out on, or sidestep, the personal agony and ecstasy of feeling that pulses

31

and flows behind and between the cut-and-dried demonstrable facts.

The Rational Mind

Some Geminis must have names and explanations for everything they come across. They'll deny a thing is real unless they have experienced it themselves, or it fits in with their own model of joined-up thinking. Favourites for binning are ideals, emotions, the irrational and blind faith without proof. Geminis like this can be very difficult to deal with because of their slickness in justifying their own mental defensiveness and intellectual rigidity.

Most Geminis, though, are acutely aware of the deeper mysteries of life and that there are more things in heaven and earth than are dreamt of in any philosophy. But these flashes of insight can be disturbing and sometimes downright unwelcome. When you don't understand something or can't order it in your rational mind, you can feel out of your depth and in danger of being swamped. Sometimes it's hard to know whether you are a scientist or a mystic, an artist or an intellectual. Whenever you're doing one thing, another part of you wants to move on and do something else. It's hard to bear the tension of staying present at the place you are in. Your challenge is not to take sides with one part of your personality against the other but to learn to translate what goes on in one half of your experience into the language of the other – masculine and feminine, logic and intuition, intimacy and freedom, good and evil, capitalism and communism. Then, with a foot in both camps, you can move from an either–or to a both–and situation. This will give you the very best of both worlds and heal the split at the heart of Gemini.

Many fine mediums, like Alice Bailey, have Gemini

strong in their charts. Sir Arthur Conan Doyle, creator of the ultra-rational Sherlock Holmes, was a zealous convert to spiritualism in later life. Apparently he made a disembodied visit after his death to speak through the medium Grace Cooke to set the record straight, saying that a lot of spiritualist teaching was, in fact, wide of the mark.

Social Polish

You don't cope well with solitude. A desert island is probably not for you, no matter how many discs and books you could take with you. You long for the closeness of human company. Even just knowing that there is someone there in the next room can be immensely reassuring. As you're naturally sociable and gregarious, being left out or overlooked when anything new is happening just doesn't bear thinking about. With your polished social skills, impeccable manners and variety of interests, you can strike up an instant rapport with just about anyone, so you have plenty of acquaintances, but deepening contacts into closer, long-lasting relationships is another matter altogether. Life can feel too short to confine yourself to the few. You prefer to dip in and move on, to allow as much freedom and latitude as possible. Brilliant at working a room, you can have one eye – and half of your attention – on the person you're talking to and the other roving round to see who's next on the agenda.

Apart from the odd windbag who hogs every conversation, contributing nothing more substantial than blasts of hot air, most Geminis make delightful and warmly welcome additions to any social event. Like hummingbirds, you bring colour and cheer with your hovering presence. Hummingbirds are the only birds able to fly backwards, but they are mere amateurs when compared to you, with your ability to back-pedal out of entrapping situations. Although you'll question others about themselves and their lives with a charming curiosity that can be perilously close to nosiness, you instinctively duck and dive if the spotlight's turned on what's inside you. There's a deep-seated fear of what might be in there and, worse, that if you reveal too much of yourself you'll be pinned down in some way and lose your freedom and power to manoeuvre.

Penetrating Wit

Geminis are often gifted at sophisticated satire and smart repartee. You can be a wonderful mimic, imitating accents and summing up your victim in a few deft gestures. Because you're rarely pompous and have a sense of the ridiculous, you can laugh at yourself too. Wit has been said to lie in the likeness of things that are different, and in the difference of things that are alike. That's just right up your street and why you're so good at it. Clever puns are your speciality, and with your sharp memory for phrases and fragments, you love peppering the conversation with fitting quotations.

Life's Ups and Downs

Like the mercury in thermometers and barometers, your mind responds instantly to circulating changes in mental temperature and pressure so you can be inconsistent and prone to mood swings. A depressing thought can have you sinking into the depths of despondency, while an uplifting one will have you vivacious and sparkling in an instant. This can make you seem fickle and unstable, even to yourself. One minute you're high as a kite – happy, smiling, chatty, friendly and wide open to life – the next you've abruptly turned cold and even cynical. You may even cut off contact with friends and withdraw into yourself. Then just as suddenly – and for no apparent reason – you can pull yourself together and are back to your usual happy, laughing self again. It's important that you can find some way of reassuring those you care about that these withdrawals are not personal, or it can cause endless misunderstandings and, often, hurt.

Gemini at Work

You may prefer to have two or more jobs, rather than confine yourself to just one. Many Geminis are Jacks and Jills of all trades and masterful at some. Others chop and change career and never settle down, then feel guilty and uneasy because they have been told that's wrong. But wrong for whom? Anything that demands routine, monotony or being forced to sit still will drive you crazy, though you'd almost certainly do a disappearing trick long before things got to that stage. Working alone is simply not for you. If, for any reason, you have to, one thing's certain – your telephone bill will be astronomical. You're perfectly happy to take orders and work under supervision because that means that someone else carries the final responsibility, something you're usually delighted to do without. You do, however, prefer to work at a job in your own way, as you're an ace at finding shortcuts, and like to have some freedom to come and go when you please. Flexi-time working hours could suit you well.

Cutting a Deal

Communication is your speciality, as you're superb at making connections, both socially and mentally. Any job which allows you to get out and about and meet a wide variety of new people, for short periods of time, could be just the ticket for you. Because you're so persuasive and charming and can make buying anything seem perfectly logical and utterly irresistible, you're a natural at sales and promotions. As an agent or middleman or woman, you're hard to beat. It's here that your mobility and wide-ranging interests and experience really come into their own. Bringing together people and things which, on the surface, seem to have nothing in common and making creative connections is what you do naturally. To get paid for it as well is icing on the cake. The media, especially journalism and publishing, is a hive abuzz with Geminis. Education, psychology and science are other fertile fields for you and, as you may be skilled at languages, being a translator or interpreter could be a good career choice too.

The Healthy Gemini

Your youthful outlook is an enormous health bonus and because you move around so much, using up bags of nervous energy, you're unlikely to become fat. However, your tendency to have too many irons in far too many fires can have you spreading yourself so thin that you risk running yourself ragged, ending up highly strung and jumpy. Difficulty in chilling out and relaxing can lead to insomnia and even nervous exhaustion, but lack of mental stimulation, for you, can be much worse. One Gemini I know, with a boring job, ended up at the doctor's with symptoms of stress. Though you'll hide it well, some Geminis can become obsessive about health, but bottle their fears up and never tell a soul. It's here that a problem shared can be a problem halved, as often the main problem is simply the worry itself. A quiet talk with a relaxed partner and a long, slow massage can soothe your frazzled wiring – if you'll just lie still long enough to let it take effect.

Gemini rules the brain and nervous system, as well as the lungs, arms, hands and shoulders. When under stress, you could be susceptible to respiratory or thyroid problems and eating too quickly, talking all the while and not taking time to chew input properly – edible or emotional – can lead to digestive upsets. Some Geminis have a tendency to stiff joints, aggravated by dry and windy weather. Excess sunlight, computer and television radiation and information overload can make any existing health problems worse. Geminis often love to try out all the latest advances and fads in healthcare. To keep well, you need lots of rest and fresh air, as well as physical exercise, and contact sports like judo, aikido and dancing can be especially helpful.

No Ties, Please

You're fun to be with, but fickle, and love to flirt, keeping situations light. Your ability to strike up an instant rapport with just about anybody can be misinterpreted as a come-on or an invitation to deepen the relationship. Usually it's nothing of the sort – you're just curious and experimenting. Most Geminis prefer to see themselves as upright and ethical so your choice would be to stay above board and truthful in relationships. Sometimes, however, your emotional intelligence doesn't match your love of analysis and you can come out with the most inappropriate things – like how much you fancy that person over there. You may be able to uncouple your feelings from an interesting observation like that but it's unlikely that your partner is going to appreciate it in quite the same way. You may need to learn that truth is a delicate matter and a great deal more subtle than a series of neatly arranged facts. You can be expert at disguising your true feelings –

even from yourself – which makes it hard to be emotionally honest. Being so afraid of being tied down, you can play down or ignore the fact that you care for someone deeply.

Because you're curious, you can enjoy sexual experimentation – and, especially when young, the novelty of lots of different partners, in your head as fantasy, if not in your bed in the flesh. Sex for you, unless you have some raunchier components in your chart, can be fairly impersonal, more like a wonderfully pleasurable shared work-out with someone you like than an opportunity for steamy passion. For your partner, depending on their particular astro-mix, this can feel either like a painful rejection or a welcome relief from messy emotions.

Fear of Feelings

Relationships are often a bit of a minefield for you. Being more at home in the world of ideas, physical and emotional intimacy can feel quite threatening and many Geminis find physical affection uncomfortable. Even hugs for some are hard to handle. You may enjoy discussing feelings but aren't over-keen on confronting the genuine article, in either yourself or your partners – largely because you're not sure how to deal with them, and they can feel so overwhelming. Some Geminis prefer to avoid emotional maturity altogether and drift into Peter Pan and Wendy relationships, where their partners look after them indulgently, overlooking inconsiderate and irresponsible behaviour and allowing them to dodge the pain of having to grow up.

Marriage of Minds

Only when there's a real meeting of minds can you become emotionally involved. If you can't communicate well with your partner, it's a non-starter. Despite Geminis' reputation for being run-arounds, you are perfectly capable of being faithful and making a lasting commitment – provided, of course, that your partner remembers the following: if you love someone, set them free. If they come back to you, they are yours. If not, they never were in the first place.

SIX

Aspects of the Sun

PLANETS, JUST LIKE PEOPLE, CAN HAVE IMPORTANT RELATIONSHIPS with each other. These relationships are called aspects. Aspects to your Sun from any other planet can influence your personality markedly. The most powerful effects come with those from the slower-moving planets – Saturn, Uranus, Neptune or Pluto. Sometimes they can alter your ideas about yourself and your behaviour patterns so much that you may not feel at all typical of your sign in certain areas of your life.

Check if your birth date and year appear in the various sections below to find out if one or more of these planets was aspecting the Sun when you were born. Only the so-called challenging aspects have been included. These are formed when the planets are together, opposite or at right angles to each other in the sky.

Unfortunately, because space is restricted, other aspects have been left out, although they have similar effects to those described below and, for the same reason, a few dates will inevitably have been missed out, too. (You can find out for sure whether or not your Sun is aspected at my website www.janeridderpatrick.com) If your Sun has no aspects to

Saturn, Uranus, Neptune or Pluto, you're more likely to be a typical Gemini.

Some well-known Geminis with challenging aspects to their Suns appear below. You can find more in the birthday section at the end of the book.

Gemini Sun in Aspect with Saturn

If you were born between 1942 and 1944, 1971 and 1973 or 2000 and 2003, whether or not your birthday is listed below, you are likely to feel the influence of Saturn on your Sun.

21 May–1 June in: 1934–5, 1942–3, 1949, 1956–7, 1964, 1971–2, 1978–9, 1986 and 1993–4

2 June–11 June in: 1935–6, 1943, 1950, 1957, 1965, 1979–80, 1987, 1994

12 June–22 June in: 1936–7, 1944, 1951, 1958–9, 1966, 1973–4, 1987–8 and 1995–6

Richard Dimbleby	Venus Williams	Josephine Baker
Prince Philip	Anne Frank	Elizabeth Hurley

Saturn is the planet of limits and obligations, neither of which has much appeal for freewheeling Gemini. There can be a constant tug-of-war between your sense of responsibility and your longing to skip off and play. When your Gemini Sun is winning, you can feel like a naughty child thumbing your nose at the grown-ups, which often attracts raps over the knuckles from people in authority. When Saturn has the upper hand, you may be aware of a critic inside your head making discouraging and disparaging comments, especially about your academic abilities, communication skills or general competence. These echo the 'oughts' and 'shoulds' that you picked up early in life and sometimes, if you examine yourself honestly, you might spot that you could be setting yourself up to be disapproved of for these very inadequacies – quite unnecessarily. Some become self-critical and ambitious high achievers, driven by the need to win approval from the world. Others keep putting off doing anything because they are scared to put themselves to the test.

Your early years may have been tough or harsh, possibly through material, educational or emotional deprivation, or high parental expectations. Although royalty, Prince Philip's childhood was no bed of roses, Josephine Baker was raised in bleak poverty and Anne Frank's restrictions were literal and physical. This difficult start can fuel a powerful ambition to make something of your life. Real contentment comes when you stop looking for outside validation, set your own standards and goals, then put your nose to the grindstone and work to speak with authority yourself. You may not, like commentator Richard Dimbleby, become the Voice of the Nation. But, in your own way, you can become a respected spokesperson in whatever field your interest lies.

Gemini Sun in Aspect with Uranus

If you were born between 1942 and 1948, whether or not your birthday is listed below, you are likely to feel the influence of Uranus on your Sun.

21 May–1 June in: 1941–5, 1962–6 and 1981–4
2–11 June in: 1944–7, 1965–8 and 1983–7
12–22 June in: 1946–50, 1967–70 and 1986–9

Patch Adams	Richard Wagner	Judy Garland
Salman Rushdie	Bob Dylan	W.B. Yeats

Uranus is the rattler of bars, the breaker of moulds and the herald of progress. It has very little time or respect for tradition or the status quo, and neither have you. You tend to be ahead of your time and often out of step with what the common herd thinks today. Although your ideas can appear completely off the wall, or unacceptably shocking, in the course of time what was so innovative and strange when you first came up with it often becomes absorbed into mainstream thinking and is then considered just plain common sense. The trouble with being ahead of your time, or out of step, is that some people feel threatened by change and would happily shoot the messenger – fortunately rarely as literally as in the case of Salman Rushdie, whose book *The Satanic Verses*, seen as blasphemous, earned him a death threat.

Conventional careers and conventional commitments may be difficult, if not downright impossible, for you and with a strong streak of unpredictability you're unlikely always to be the easiest person to get along with. Richard Wagner wrote ground-breaking opera, yet even his close friends found his behaviour almost unbearable – meddling in political revolutions, outrageous extravagance, stubborn egotism and highly scandalous love affairs. You're a trailblazer and iconoclast; you're not a conformist. American doctor Patch Adams never charges patients and maintains that humour is more important than drugs or therapy. He often sees patients dressed as a clown to cheer them up. You may not reach the heights of eccentricity of Wagner and Adams, but somewhere, somehow, you'll be out of the ordinary. Learning to switch off is vital; your nervous system is likely to be on overdrive. The art is to find a lifestyle that caters for both you and those around you.

Gemini Sun in Aspect with Neptune

21 May–1 June in: 1929–35 and 1969–76
2–11 June in: 1934–40 and 1974–81
12–22 June in: 1938–45 and 1978–85

Naomi Campbell	Jamie Oliver	Joan Collins
Paul McCartney	M.C. Escher	Colleen McCullough

Gemini is the sign of the trend-spotter, while Neptune is the planet of yearning for bliss. Put the two together and you have a merchant of dreams. You instinctively tap into what the world wants and know how to package and present it skilfully. Calculating and planning is rarely how you operate; you are more of a medium or mouthpiece for a message that speaks through you. Paul McCartney, with the Beatles, was the embodiment of the magical mood of the '60s. It's not always easy to know who you are when you're not in role. Unless there are more stabilising factors in your chart, there's a danger that you can get caught up in believing your own hype and over-estimating your own importance; alternatively you could be dogged by vague feelings of emptiness or worthlessness – or swing between the two extremes. It is important for you to find an ideal bigger than your own ego that you can serve. Then you can live out the very finest potential of this aspect – making a selfless contribution to helping the less fortunate to lead a better life. You may need to learn to say no – firmly. Being so acutely aware of suffering and neediness, you tend to take on too much because you easily feel guilty and over-responsible for rescuing others. You may be drawn to partners or father-substitutes that you put on a pedestal, or who are in some way unavailable. If so, cut them a bit of slack and allow them some human failings or your own unrealistic expectations could lead to disappointment. Escape from everyday reality has immense appeal so do take care, when the going gets rough, not to escape into alcohol or food, as you are prone to excesses.

Gemini Sun in Aspect with Pluto

21 May–1 June in: 1957–65
2–11 June in: 1962–9
12–22 June in: 1967–73

Katharine Graham	Harriet Beecher Stowe	Mary Whitehouse
Lord Beaverbrook	Norman Vincent Peale	Elizabeth Hurley

'When you get into a tight place and everything goes against you, till it seems you could not hold on a minute longer, never give up then, for that is just the place and time that the tide will turn,' wrote Harriet Beecher Stowe, author of *Uncle Tom's Cabin* – excellent advice for anyone with Pluto aspecting their Sun, because you can bet your bottom dollar that tight places will present themselves to you, in one form or another, throughout your life. You may find yourself scapegoated or hitting rock bottom or feeling compelled to confront the misuse of power. Mary Whitehouse stood firmly by her principles, despite blistering ridicule, in her campaign against what she saw as the corrupting influence of pornography and violence on television. Katharine Graham of *The Washington Post* exposed President Nixon's involvement and cover-up in Watergate, despite threats to her well-being and livelihood. Tough though this aspect can be, if you hold fast to what you believe to be true, you will find untold resources within yourself to pull through. Pluto is the planet of transformation. Its agenda is to eliminate anything that stands in the way of survival. Your choice is to decide what it is you want to survive – good or evil – and to know the difference between the two. As you don't find it easy to trust, often because of early experiences of feeling unwanted, you may be rather secretive and self-protective. If you feel betrayed, you could tend to brood, which plays havoc with your sensitive nervous system. Don't forget that the best revenge is to live well. Remember too the title of Norman Vincent Peale's bestseller *The Power of Positive Thinking* – that attitude will stand you in good stead through good times and hard.

SEVEN

Meeting Your Moon

☽THE GLYPH FOR THE MOON IS THE SEMI-CIRCLE OR CRESCENT. It is a symbol for the receptiveness of the soul and is associated with feminine energies and the ebb and flow of the rhythms of life. In some Islamic traditions it represents the gateway to paradise and the realms of bliss.

The Sun and Moon are the two complementary poles of your personality, like yang and yin, masculine and feminine, active and reflective, career and home, father and mother. The Moon comes into its own as a guide at night, the time of sleeping consciousness. It also has a powerful effect on the waters of the earth. Likewise, the Moon in your birth chart describes what you respond to instinctively and feel 'in your waters', often just below the level of consciousness. It is your private radar system, sending you messages via your body responses and feelings, telling you whether a situation seems safe or scary, nice or nasty. Feelings provide vital information about circumstances in and around you. Ignore them at your peril; that will lead you into emotional, and sometimes even physical, danger. Eating disorders tend to be associated with being out of touch with, or neglecting, the instincts and the body, both of which the Moon describes.

Extraordinary though it might seem to those who are emotionally tuned in, some people have great difficulty in knowing what they are feeling. One simple way is to pay attention to your body. Notice any sensations that attract your attention. Those are linked to your feelings. Now get a sense of whether they are pleasant or unpleasant, then try to put a more exact name to what those feelings might be. Is it sadness, happiness, fear? What is it that they are trying to tell you? Your Moon hints at what will strongly activate your feelings. Learning to trust and decode this information will help make the world seem – and be – a safer place.

The Moon represents your drive to nurture and protect yourself and others. Its sign, house and aspects describe how you respond and adapt emotionally to situations and what feeds you, in every sense of the word. It gives information about your home and home life and how you experienced your mother, family and childhood, as well as describing your comfort zone of what feels familiar – the words 'family' and 'familiar' come from the same source. It shows, too, what makes you feel secure and what could comfort you when you're feeling anxious. Your Moon describes what moves and motivates you powerfully at the deepest instinctual level and indicates what is truly the 'matter' in – or with – your life.

Knowing children's Moon signs can help parents and teachers better understand their insecurities and respect their emotional make-up and needs, and so prevent unnecessary hurt, or even harm, to sensitive young lives. It's all too easy to expect that our children and parents should have the same emotional wiring as we do, but that's rarely how life works. Finding our parents' Moon signs can be a real revelation. It can often help us understand where they are coming from, what they need and why they react to us in the way they do. Many of my clients have been able to find the understanding and compassion to forgive their parents when they realised that they were doing their very best with the emotional resources available to them.

In relationships it is important that your Moon's requirements are met to a good enough extent. For example, if you have your Moon in Sagittarius you must have adventure, freedom and the opportunity to express your beliefs. If being with your partner constantly violates these basic needs, you will never feel secure and loved and the relationship could, in the long term, undermine you. However, if your Moon feels too comfortable, you will never change and grow. The art is to get a good working balance between support and challenge.

A man's Moon sign can show some of the qualities he will unconsciously select in a wife or partner. Some of the others are shown in his Venus sign. Many women can seem much more like their Moon signs than their Sun signs, especially if they are involved in mothering a family and being a support system for their husbands or partners. It is only at the mid-life crisis that many women start to identify more with the qualities of their own Suns rather than living that out through their partners' ambitions. Similarly, men tend to live out the characteristics of their Moon signs through their wives and partners until mid-life, often quite cut off from their own feelings and emotional responses. If a man doesn't seem at all like his Moon sign, then check out the women in his life. There's a good chance that his wife, mother or daughter will show these qualities.

Your Moon can be in any sign, including the same one as your Sun. Each sign belongs to one of the four elements: Fire, Earth, Air or Water. The element of your Moon can give you a general idea of how you respond to new situations and what you need to feel safe and comforted. We all become anxious if our Moon's needs are not being recognised and attended to. We then, automatically, go into our personal little rituals for making ourselves feel better. Whenever you are feeling distressed, especially when you are way out of your comfort zone in an unfamiliar situation, do something to feed and soothe your Moon. You're almost certain to calm down quickly.

Fire Moons

If you have a fire Moon in Aries, Leo or Sagittarius, your first response to any situation is to investigate in your imagination the possibilities for drama, excitement and self-expression. Feeling trapped by dreary routine in an ordinary humdrum life crushes you completely. Knowing that you are carrying out a special mission feeds your soul. To you, all the world's a stage and a voyage of discovery. Unless you are at the centre of the action playing some meaningful role, anxiety and depression can set in. To feel secure, you have to have an appropriate outlet for expressing your spontaneity, honourable instincts and passionate need to be of unqiue significance. The acknowledgement, appreciation and feedback of people around you are essential, or you don't feel real. Not to be seen and appreciated, or to be overlooked, can feel like a threat to your very existence.

Earth Moons

If you have an earth Moon in Taurus, Virgo or Capricorn, you'll respond to new situations cautiously and practically. Rapidly changing circumstances where you feel swept along and out of control are hard for you to cope with. You need time for impressions to sink in. Sometimes it is only much later, after an event has taken place, that you become sure what you felt about it. Your security lies in slowing down, following familiar routines and rituals, even if they are a bit obsessive, and focusing on something, preferably material – possibly the body itself or nature – which is comforting because it is still there. Indulging the senses in some way often helps too, through food, sex or body care. So does taking charge of the practicalities of the immediate situation, even if this is only mixing the drinks or passing out clipboards. To feel secure, you need continuity and a sense that you have your hand on the rudder of your own life. Think of the rather irreverent joke about the man seeming to cross himself in a crisis, all the while actually touching his most valued possessions to check that they are still intact – spectacles, testicles, wallet and watch. That must have been thought up by someone with the Moon in an earth sign.

Air Moons

When your Moon is in an air sign – Gemini, Libra or Aquarius – you feel most secure when you can stand back from situations and observe them from a distance. Too much intimacy chokes you and you'll tend to escape it by going into your head to the safety of ideas and analysis. Even in close relationships you need your mental, and preferably physical, space. You often have to think, talk or write about what you are feeling before you are sure what your feelings are. By putting them 'out there' so that you can examine them clearly, you can claim them as your own. Unfairness and unethical behaviour can upset you badly and make you feel uneasy until you have done something about it or responded in some way. It can be easy with an air Moon to be unaware of, or to ignore, your own feelings because you are more responsive to ideas, people and situations outside of yourself that may seem to have little connection with you. This is not a good idea, as it cuts you off from the needs of your body as well as your own emotional intelligence. Making opportunities to talk, play with and exchange ideas and information can reduce the stress levels if anxiety strikes.

Water Moons

Finally, if your Moon is in a water sign – Cancer, Scorpio or Pisces – you are ultra-sensitive to atmospheres, and you can experience other people's pain or distress as if they were your own. You tend to take everything personally and, even if the situation has nothing at all to do with you, feel responsible for making it better. Your worst nightmare is to feel no emotional response coming back from other people. That activates your deep-seated terror of abandonment, which can make you feel that you don't exist and is, quite literally, what you fear even more than death. If you feel insecure, you may be tempted to resort to emotional manipulation to try to force intimacy with others – not a good idea, as this can lead to the very rejection that you dread. You are at your most secure when the emotional climate is positive and you have trusted, supportive folk around who will winkle you out of hiding if you become too reclusive. With a water Moon, it is vital to learn to value your own feelings and to take them seriously – and to have a safe, private place you can retreat to when you feel emotionally fragile. As you never forget anything which has made a feeling impression on you, sometimes your reactions are triggered by unconscious memories of things long past, rather than what is taking place in the present. When you learn to interpret them correctly, your feelings are your finest ally and will serve you well.

Finding Your Moon Sign

If you don't yet know your Moon sign, before looking it up, you could have some fun reading through the descriptions that follow and seeing if you can guess which one it is. To find your Moon sign, check your year and date of birth in the tables on pp. 99–112. For a greater in-depth understanding of your Moon sign, you might like to read about its characteristics in the book in this series about that sign.

At the beginning of each section are the names of some well-known Geminis with that particular Moon sign. You can find more about them in Chapter Ten.

Sun in Gemini with Moon in Aries

Delia Smith	Isadora Duncan	Gilbert Harding
Jeffrey Dahmer	Jackie Stewart	Alastair Campbell

The gift of an Aries Moon is energy and focus. You've a passion for life that can be truly uplifting. You believe in yourself and your projects totally and throw yourself into them with gusto. While your Gemini Sun is easily distracted, not so your Moon. That means business. You can be an inspired, and inspiring, leader and a first-class promoter. You are at your best starting off enterprises, spearheading campaigns and putting your own spin on matters. Then, when the ground has been broken and the excitement has died down – and the inevitable tangle of red tape creeps in to engulf you – it's time to move on to something more scintillating. You're great at setting armies marching, not stuck at a desk administrating. Tied down, you'd either implode or explode.

With an appetite for action, risk-taking turns you on.

It's important to have some worthwhile cause or challenge into which you can pour all of that dynamic energy. For some, like Jackie Stewart, the racing driver, this can be physical. More often, though, the war is fought with words. Gilbert Harding, the outspoken TV and radio presenter of *The Brains Trust* and *Round Britain Quiz*, became a household name as 'the rudest man in Britain' and often bullied guests on his shows if they gave evasive answers.

Your challenge is to find the courage to have your own needs met, being neither aggressive yourself nor intimidated by others. Serial killer Jeffrey Dahmer failed in this spectacularly. He carried out fifteen gruesome murders of homosexual men, mutilating and eating his victims, quite literally feeding on violence. He was himself later bludgeoned to death in prison. Much better that all that energy at your disposal – which needs to find an outlet – be used wisely and well!

Sun in Gemini with Moon in Taurus

Bjorn Borg	Joan Collins	Ian Fleming
King Charles II	Isabella Rossellini	Kristin Scott Thomas

A sentence in a biography of Charles II begins 'Charles' propensity for debauchery . . .'. Now, I'm not suggesting for a minute that all Gemini Sun–Taurus Moon people lead lascivious lives, but with your love of variety and appetite for the sensual, it could be an option. I know several people with this mix whose wildly entertaining stories of their sexual adventures – and ingenuity of places selected to carry them out – have astonished and delighted their friends over the years. Yes, I'm afraid there can be an element of kiss-and-tell here, unless discretion or secrecy is indicated elsewhere in your chart. What's the point of having fun if you can't share it round? Ian Fleming's gimmick-loving hero, James Bond, is a perfect example of a lothario of this kind. Yet Taurus loves stability and you are perfectly capable of loyal and lasting long-term relationships, if there is enough variety and mental stimulation in the partnership to compensate for passing up on opportunities to stray.

It's a rare person with a Moon in Taurus who doesn't enjoy being in control of all they survey and you're unlikely to be an exception. One thing you do insist on is regular refuelling, preferably of the gourmet kind. Too long between mealtimes can make you irritable. Beauty nourishes you, and you may enjoy pampering yourself to ensure you always look your best. A healthy bank balance and a home that you own, preferably with a garden, are necessities, not luxuries. Change that happens too fast can completely unnerve you so when the pace becomes hectic it's time to slow down and relax. Music, peaceful pottering and communing with nature are just what's needed then to restore frazzled nerves.

Sun in Gemini with Moon in Gemini

Sir Christopher Bland　M.C. Escher　　　Kylie Minogue
Dorothy L. Sayers　　Queen Victoria　Rebekah Wade

Pens and ink, phones and emails could have been invented with you in mind. If you can't communicate, share and comment on your experiences, it's like being starved of oxygen. Queen Victoria kept a daily diary documenting her thoughts from the age of 13 and ploughed through acres of state paperwork, insisting on frequent consultations with ministers, while managing to keep up a voluminous correspondence with her equally voluminous and far-flung family, on matters great and small. Even a queen, with this combo, loves a good gossip.

You make an excellent reporter, communicator, writer and mimic, as you are quick to pick up the essence of what is going on and pass it on to others with a few deft words or gestures. Paradoxes and playing tricks with words and images delights you, though you may not be as slick as M.C. Escher, whose drawings of ascending and descending waterfalls and impossible buildings show how plausibly a few artful strokes can deceive the eyes and the mind. You probably drove parents and teachers crazy with your relentless curiosity and questions and constant hopping from one topic to the next. Sir Christopher Bland, Chairman of the Board of Governors of the BBC, was accused by a friend of having the attention span of a peanut. In the excitement of the moment, it's sometimes tempting to skim superficially and just allow what's around you to flow in through your eyes, ears and senses and out of your mouth or keyboard with only a cursory editing by consciousness. Being so wired to the pulse of what's of the minute, even the minimum of mental discipline can make you a superb commentator, earning you great respect.

Gemini Sun with Moon in Cancer

Lord Beaverbrook	Boy George	Tom Jones
Thomas Hardy	Enoch Powell	Nancy Sinatra

Being more intuitive than you probably recognise, you can pick up instantly on both emotional atmospheres and what is currently of popular interest – quite an asset if you work with the public. Lord Beaverbrook took the world of journalism by storm when he turned the *Daily Express* into the most widely read daily newspaper in the world through a combination of clever promotion and supplying what he sensed the masses wanted. You feel deeply and are easily moved to tears by any strong sentiment and may try to suppress this firmly, as you could find it embarrassing. Problems can arise when you don't recognise that you pick up *everyone's* feelings and not just your own. This means that, at times, especially when tired, you can become touchy and take offence where none is intended, then allow resentment to fester and eat away at you. When that happens, switching in to your Gemini logic will get things back into proportion.

Feeling connected to your roots or family is vital for your sense of security. One of Tom Jones's keynote songs is 'The Green, Green Grass of Home'. Unlike cosmopolitan Gemini, clannish Cancer can be parochial and patriotic, dividing the world into 'us' and 'them' and being deeply suspicious of 'them'. Enoch Powell spoke out against immigration into Britain from Africa and Asia, saying that it filled him with foreboding. Some with Cancer Moons who have felt betrayed or hurt, especially in childhood, put up impenetrable emotional barricades and can even become cruel. Most, however, are closely attached to mother and home, sometimes too much for their partners' comfort. Because it can be hard for you to admit to yourself just how emotionally dependent you can be, you can strenuously deny it, but allowing appropriate intimacy into your life will enhance it beyond measure.

Gemini Sun with Moon in Leo

| Kathy Burke | Helena Bonham Carter | Jacques Cousteau |
| Anne Frank | Rudolph Giuliani | Paul McCartney |

With the Moon in royal Leo, you're well aware that you are the centre of your universe and star of your own fast-shifting, kaleidoscopic show. Plenty of attention from others is essential or you can become quite insecure. Some with this combination, with no outlet for performing, complete with appreciative audience applause, slip into attention-seeking behaviour and upstaging others to feed their need. You hate to be seen in a poor light but sometimes, especially if your pride is ruffled, you can be a tad overbearing. You urgently need an honourable role to play, where it is appropriate for you to stand in the spotlight radiating generosity, leadership, service and integrity. Mayor Giuliani of New York was widely unpopular, despite his tough and successful stance on crime, until after the terrorists attacks on the city on 11 September 2001. In the terrible aftermath, he seemed to be everywhere at once, lifting hearts and spirits, a tireless figurehead available at every hour of the day or night for anyone in distress. When you learn to respect the needs of others and give generously of your time and self, for the sheer joy of it, expecting nothing in return, you are truly stellar and reap rich rewards of love gladly returned.

Any career which combines performing and communicating is right up your street. This is a first-class combination for teachers, actors and writers, where charisma and communication skills are highly prized. Sometimes a Leo Moon indicates that you come from a prominent family or have a powerful, dramatic and possibly domineering mother or – for men – wife. It certainly means that you are at your best in a home you can be proud of.

Sun in Gemini with Moon in Virgo

Courteney Cox	Paul Gauguin	John F. Kennedy
Peggy Lee	Mary Whitehouse	Frank Lloyd Wright

With the double Mercury influence – Mercury rules both Gemini and Virgo – you're skilled at finding ingenious solutions to practical problems. You've a knack of analysing a situation meticulously, penetrating to the essence of what needs fixing and coming up with the most effective and efficient way forward. You can be skilled at turning your eye for detail and love of the useful to good commercial effect, like Frank Lloyd Wright with his innovative, yet highly practical, architectural designs. Whatever you do, you like to do it well. It's soothing for you to focus on just one task at a time and deal with that thoroughly before going on to the next. Too much sensory input can be overwhelming, so it's important to say 'enough' when the warning signs of this start to appear. You respond well to a pure diet and a simple daily routine, and you may also have an interest in body care and healthy living.

Sloppiness, especially in thinking, can drive you to distraction. With your ability to spot a flaw at 100 paces, you've a highly critical mind, and often a tongue to match. Hopefully, though, you don't take your nit-picking to such neurotic extremes as Courteney Cox's character, Monica, in the TV sitcom *Friends*. Your nervous system is highly strung, so quiet time alone for reflection is essential. Some with this mix can get bogged down in detail, but most of you tend to focus on those few areas that interest you at the time, and the rest you'll just ignore. You may hanker after the innocent purity of a simple life, like the painter Gauguin who turned his back on the civilisation that he hated and went to live on a South Sea island.

Gemini Sun with Moon in Libra

Stanley Baxter   Benazir Bhutto Tony Curtis
Henry Kissinger Wallis Simpson Edward Elgar

Even if you're a small-town kid, you probably stand out for your cosmopolitan style and meticulous grooming. Men with this Moon usually like and understand women, don't feel threatened by femininity and may in fact prefer women's company to men's. Stanley Baxter, in his stunning television extravaganzas, took the combination of Gemini wit and mimicry and Libran elegance to new heights. His stunning frocks and superb legs were the envy of most women, and many men too. Women with Libra Moons often have a steeliness of resolve under a charming exterior, and refuse to stay put in a 'woman's role'. Benazir Bhutto, the strikingly attractive ex-prime minister of Pakistan, managed to rise to the top in her powerfully male-dominated world.

Fairness matters to you. This can make you a first-class diplomat, as you can listen to everybody's point of view and find just the right words to soothe ruffled feelings. If there is an atmosphere of disharmony around, or you sense that you have offended someone, you won't feel comfortable till you've patched it up. This drive for balance, plus formidable negotiating skills, can help you mend rifts between others – as did Henry Kissinger, who won the Nobel Peace Prize for helping improve relations between both China and Russia and the Arabs and Israelis. However, if everything is becoming too nice and cosy, you can stir up trouble with a charming smile. For you, too nice is just as unbalanced as too nasty.

You are not responsible for the world's hurts and injustices, nor are you duty-bound to broker the healing of them all. It's imortant to pay attention to creating your own happiness too. It's only fair, after all . . .

Sun in Gemini with Moon in Scorpio

| G.K. Chesterton | Earl Haig | Xaviera Hollander |
| Elizabeth Hurley | Alanis Morissette | Priscilla Presley |

Sex, death, mysteries, suspicion and power are the abiding themes of your life. Xaviera Hollander, brothel-owner and sexual experimenter, who wrote her million-selling autobiography *The Happy Hooker*, made a career out of them. Others are involved in life-and-death struggles, as was Earl Haig, Commander-in-Chief of the British Army in France in the First World War, who fought battles of brutal butchery on the front, as well as against back-stabbing attempts at home to try to undermine him. His belief in the afterlife, confirmed by dead friends at seances, gave him the strength to carry on until he achieved victory. Like him, you have deep reserves of emotional power that come to your aid when your back is to the wall. You may surprise even yourself with how resourceful a survivor you are, and how threat can bring out the best, or worst, in you.

You are capable of loyal and long-lasting relationships but if your trust is ever betrayed you may forgive . . . but forget? Never! Nor are you likely to let the culprit forget either. Occasionally, the scorpion's tail can lash out with a vengeance. When a driver with a shiny new Porsche tried to get too pushy with one Gemini–Scorpio woman, she deliberately ran her suitcase over the bonnet, leaving an expensive souvenir of deep parallel scratches. Not nice, but some people, you might argue, could do with a taste of their own medicine. There are more constructive ways, however, of living out a Scorpio Moon, exploring and airing the darker side of life, helping to reveal corruption or cruelty and heal emotional wounds. The art is to learn to trust life even when there appear to be no grounds for doing so.

Sun in Gemini with Moon in Sagittarius

Patch Adams	Naomi Campbell	Judy Garland
Nicole Kidman	Salvatore Ferragamo	Donald Trump

You like your life sunny side up. No matter how tough the going gets, there's part of you that remains an eternal optimist. Right now, it may be rainy and grey. You can feel lonely, depressed and miserable – but, like Judy Garland's Dorothy, in *The Wizard of Oz*, you cling to the hope that there is somewhere over the rainbow where the world glows in vibrant colours and all is well – and that that place could be just around the corner.

Throwing caution to the winds, you plunge straight in with enthusiasm to whatever adventure beckons you. You can be recklessly extravagant and sometimes your taste is less than restrained. Property tycoon Donald Trump has been known to overgild the lily from time to time in his palatial residences. There is nothing small or mean-minded about a Sagittarius Moon. You can be generous to a fault, for you rarely count the cost. Why should you? You live on the assumption that supply is unlimited and anyway, unless caution is writ large somewhere else in your chart, worrying about limitations and responsibilities is somebody else's business.

You hate to be confined and enjoy getting out and about, checking out new places, people and possibilities. You've a knack of spotting significance and potential in all that comes your way. This can make you a gifted entrepreneur, like high-fashion shoemaker Salvatore Ferragamo, or a natural philosopher. Being both a perpetual student and a life-long teacher – sometimes preacher – giving advice comes as easy as breathing. You can be an inspired coach, encouraging others to reach for the stars. Like Patch Adams, clowning and horseplay can help you express your love of fun. Being a wandering troubadour would have suited you perfectly.

Sun in Gemini with Moon in Capricorn

Margaret Drabble	Barbara Bush	King George III
Julian Clary	Dean Martin	Johnny Depp

Many with this combination have had childhoods low on either material or emotional comforts. The deprivations are often subtle. Perhaps love came with a price tag; you may have had to conform to certain strict rules of conduct and behave to suit somebody else's agenda or be responsible for looking after other family members. For one reason or another, you may have had to grow up too soon, but the good news is that it is never too late to have a happy childhood. You may have to check a tendency to be judgemental or to try to control others. George III, though a devoted father, tried to interfere excessively in the lives of his many children.

The gift of this Moon is that you are well able to look after yourself and are not afraid of hard work – in fact, it makes you feel secure. So you can turn some of that industry into creating a loving home for you and your family. Just remember to bypass the tendency to equate material security with love and to take enough time off to enjoy the fun that you need so much for a well-rounded life.

You may carry a faint air of sadness around with you, or even be prone to depression. Often the best way to handle this is to go deeper into it; you'll usually then emerge from the pit more quickly. Some cope through ironic, or black, humour. This is an award-winning combination for success in academia, the media or administration because, as well as being a skilled communicator, you are shrewd, responsible and goal-oriented. Status and upholding tradition mean a great deal to you, but you almost certainly also have a well-developed sense of mischief and the ridiculous.

Gemini Sun with Moon in Aquarius

Simon Callow	Arthur Conan Doyle	Marilyn Monroe
Jean-Paul Sartre	W.B. Yeats	Brigham Young

Your home or family background is likely to be unusual or nonconformist in some way. You may never have been quite sure that care would be continuous or reliable. Arthur Conan Doyle grew up with a mentally unstable father, with the household tiptoeing round him, trying to keep the fact secret from the outside world. Marilyn Monroe was given away by her mother and shunted between foster homes. Even if your own upbringing was outwardly stable, supportive and loving, there is likely to be something inside you that is always waiting for the rug to be pulled from under your feet, giving you the feeling that you are permanently camping. Turning this challenging Moon into a joy can mean tossing out all traditional notions of having a cosy nuclear family – that would choke you anyway – and finding new ways of creating a family unit that will work for you. Turning the idea that nowhere is secure and settled on its head, into the realisation that the whole world is your family and every woman your sister and every man your brother, can be deeply healing. You don't have to like them all. Show me a family that doesn't have its differences.

Brigham Young, leader of the Mormon community, certainly found an innovative alternative to the traditional family unit – polygamy with 17 wives and 56 children. It might not work for you, but with your Gemini versatility you've probably already come up with your own ingenious solution. You are keenly aware of injustice and you love to be involved with groups of like-minded people who aim to make the world a better place. Sometimes these groups can feel more like your family than your biological kith and kin.

Gemini Sun with Moon in Pisces

Maeve Binchy   Cilla Black   Allen Ginsberg
Colleen McCullogh Françoise Sagan Patience Strong

Part of you hates and fears confrontation of any kind and you'd often rather make light of, or ignore, difficult issues than be up-front about problems and state what you want. With your powerful need to feel at one with the world, any whiff of hostility can trigger fears of abandonment. It is important to check your tendency to brush your own needs and feelings under the carpet – pretending they don't matter won't make them go away. You'll just end up feeling hurt, guilty and resentful. Having the courage to look at tangled issues of dependency, victimhood and emotional manipulation that you're prone to encounter may be deeply healing.

You have the ability to tap into whatever feeling or longing is currently doing the rounds, and respond to it with a compassionate voice. Patience Strong did this over forty years with her uplifting verses for magazines. Though hardly great poetry, they did provide the easily digested soul food that thousands longed for. Many British soldiers went through the war with one of her comforting pieces tucked inside their pockets. Knowing that you are helping others out of their misery can give you comfort. Just be careful not to allow them to wallow – you are so susceptible to atmospheres that you can get emotionally contaminated and dragged down too. You need a place of sanctuary where you can escape from the world and all its woes, demands and distractions. It is best not to do this through overindulgence in mind-altering substances like chocolate, drugs or alcohol; you could be highly susceptible to addictions and allergies. Finding a way of accommodating both logic and a powerful spiritual yearning – whatever name you give this – is the high road to peace.

EIGHT

Mercury – It's All in the Mind

☿ THE GLYPHS FOR THE PLANETS ARE MADE UP OF THREE SYMBOLS: the circle, the semi-circle and the cross. Mercury is the only planet, apart from Pluto, whose glyph is made up of all three of these symbols. At the bottom there is the cross, representing the material world; at the top is the semi-circle of the crescent Moon, symbolising the personal soul; and in the middle, linking these two, is the circle of eternity, expressed through the individual. In mythology, Mercury was the only god who had access to all three worlds – the underworld, the middle world of earth and the higher world of the gods. Mercury in your chart represents your ability, through your thoughts and words, to make connections between the inner world of your mind and emotions, the outer world of other people and events, and the higher world of intuition. Your Mercury sign can give you a great deal of information about the way your mind works and about your interests, communication skills and your preferred learning style.

It can be frustrating when we just can't get through to some people and it's easy to dismiss them as being either completely thick or deliberately obstructive. Chances are they are neither. It may be that you're simply not talking each other's languages. Knowing your own and other people's communication styles can lead to major breakthroughs in relationships.

Information about children's natural learning patterns can help us teach them more effectively. It's impossible to learn properly if the material isn't presented in a way that resonates with the way your mind works. You just can't 'hear' it, pick it up or grasp it. Wires then get crossed and the data simply isn't processed. Many children are seriously disadvantaged if learning materials and environments don't speak to them. You may even have been a child like that yourself. If so, you could easily have been left with the false impression that you are a poor learner just because you couldn't get a handle on the lessons being taught. Identifying your own learning style can be like finding the hidden key to the treasure room of knowledge.

The signs of the zodiac are divided into four groups by element:

> The fire signs: Aries, Leo and Sagittarius
> The earth signs: Taurus, Virgo and Capricorn
> The air signs: Gemini, Libra and Aquarius
> The water signs: Cancer, Scorpio and Pisces

Your Mercury will therefore belong to one of the four elements, depending on which sign it is in. Your Mercury can only be in one of three signs – the same sign as your Sun, the one before or the one after. This means that each sign has one learning style that is never natural to it. For Gemini, this is the fire style.

Mercury in each of the elements has a distinctive way of

operating. I've given the following names to the learning and communicating styles of Mercury through the elements. Mercury in fire – active imaginative; Mercury in earth – practical; Mercury in air – logical; and Mercury in water – impressionable.

Mercury in Fire: Active Imaginative

Your mind is wide open to the excitement of fresh ideas. It responds to action and to the creative possibilities of new situations. Drama, games and storytelling are excellent ways for you to learn. You love to have fun and play with ideas. Any material to be learned has to have some significance for you personally, or add to your self-esteem, otherwise you rapidly lose interest. You learn by acting out the new information, either physically or in your imagination. The most efficient way of succeeding in any goal is to make first a mental picture of your having achieved it. This is called mental rehearsal and is used by many top sportsmen and women as a technique to help improve their performance. You do this spontaneously, as your imagination is your greatest mental asset. You can run through future scenarios in your mind's eye and see, instantly, where a particular piece of information or situation could lead and spot possibilities that other people couldn't even begin to dream of. You are brilliant at coming up with flashes of inspiration for creative breakthroughs and crisis management.

Mercury in Earth: Practical

Endless presentations of feelings, theories and possibilities can make your eyes glaze over and your brain ache to shut down. What really turns you on is trying out these theories and possibilities to see if they work in practice. If they don't, you'll tend to classify them 'of no further interest'. Emotionally charged information is at best a puzzling non-starter and at worst an irritating turn-off. Practical demonstrations, tried and tested facts and working models fascinate you. Hands-on learning, where you can see how a process functions from start to finish, especially if it leads to some useful material end-product, is right up your street. It's important to allow yourself plenty of time when you are learning, writing or thinking out what to say, otherwise you can feel rushed and out of control, never pleasant sensations for earth signs. Your special skill is in coming up with effective solutions to practical problems and in formulating long-range plans that bring concrete, measurable results.

Mercury in Air: Logical

You love learning about, and playing with, ideas, theories and principles. Often you do this best by arguing or bouncing ideas off other people, or by writing down your thoughts. Your special gift is in your ability to stand back and work out the patterns of relationship between people or things. You much prefer it when facts are presented to you logically and unemotionally and have very little time for the irrational, uncertainty or for personal opinions. You do, though, tend to have plenty of those kinds of views yourself, only you call them logical conclusions. Whether a fact is useful or not is less important than whether it fits into your mental map of how the world operates. If facts don't fit in, you'll either ignore them, find a way of making them fit, or, occasionally, make a grand leap to a new, upgraded theory. Yours is the mind of the scientist or chess player. You make a brilliant planner because you can be detached enough to take an overview of the entire situation.

Mercury in Water: Impressionable

Your mind is sensitive to atmospheres and emotional undertones and to the context in which information is presented. Plain facts and figures can often leave you cold and even intimidated. You can take things too personally and read between the lines for what you believe is really being said or taught. If you don't feel emotionally safe, you can be cautious about revealing your true thoughts. It may be hard, or even impossible, for you to learn properly in what you sense is a hostile environment. You are excellent at impression management. Like a skilful artist painting a picture, you can influence others to think what you'd like them to by using suggestive gestures or pauses and intonations. People with Mercury in water signs are often seriously disadvantaged by left-brain schooling methods that are too rigidly structured for them. You take in information best through pictures or images, so that you get a 'feel' for the material and can make an emotional bond with it, in the same way you connect with people. In emotionally supportive situations where there is a rapport between you and your instructors, or your learning material, you are able just to drink in and absorb circulating knowledge without conscious effort, sometimes not even being clear about how or why you know certain things.

Finding Your Mercury Sign

If you don't yet know your Mercury sign, you might like to see if you can guess what it is from the descriptions below before checking it out in the tables on pp. 113–15.

Sun in Gemini with Mercury in Taurus

Cilla Black	Joan Collins	Norman Vincent Peale
Alexander Pope	Brooke Shields	Richard Wagner

Your attention is drawn to anything you think will lead towards peace and stability and that gives you sensual pleasure. You have an ear for music and poetry, and a mind focused on your possessions – material, intellectual or spiritual. Your tendency to speak the plain, unvarnished truth can delight, or ruffle a few feathers, depending on who's listening.

Although you love mental stimulation, you probably agree with the poet Alexander Pope that 'a little learning is a dangerous thing' and that time, and plenty of it, is needed to check out and assimilate fresh ideas and information. You like to savour anything new with the senses for a while until it becomes familiar and you can take what you read or hear quite literally. The Gemini low threshold of boredom does not apply to your mental acquisitions. You stand loyal to those ideas that you have so carefully made your own. Once you have accepted an idea and closed your mind firmly around it, it tends to stay that way. This can be a great advantage in countering the Gemini tendency to mentally hop, skip and jump, giving you the persistence to follow through on projects and to achieve something substantial. However, if it gets to the point where you reject out of hand any ideas other than your own, you could become stubborn and inflexible, and even find plausible ways of convincing others why you are right and they are wrong. You may indeed be, but it never hurts to try out a new angle. It's hard to ditch old entrenched ideas, but when you do it tends to be sudden and complete – then you'll embrace the new with just as much tenacity as you did the old.

Sun in Gemini with Mercury in Gemini

Rachel Carson	Bob Dylan	Ian Fleming
Anne Frank	Liam Neeson	Jamie Oliver

This is the most common sign for Mercury when your Sun is in Gemini. Your mind works like greased lightning and is in tune with the latest trends that you can then, skilfully, bring to the attention of others. Gemini, along with the air signs Libra and Aquarius, normally has a strong ethical bias. Although you like to play fair, a little mischief along the way can keep things from getting too heavy. You are truly the herald and messenger of what's 'in the air', noticing what's new and passing it on. Bob Dylan was the mouthpiece for his generation's unease about the Vietnam War and other social issues. One of his best-known songs 'The Times They Are A-Changin'' just about sums up what it is you pick up and transmit. Writer Rachel Carson was well ahead of the field in alerting the world to the dangers of environmental pollution in her classic *Silent Spring*.

You have what has been referred to as a 'scientific mind' which notices facts, carefully analyses the data, matching this against what you have already seen, and then draws conclusions from what has been observed. You prefer to deal with factual evidence, reason and logic, rather than woolly-minded or sentimental thinking or irrational conclusions with no proof to back them up. You're almost always ready to try out new ideas and have a keen eye for detail in any topic that interests you. Gifted at off-the-cuff wit and repartee, you're rarely stuck for a clever answer. You may have had it said to you that you're so sharp you could cut yourself, but with your fun-loving openness and cosmopolitan tastes, you're unlikely to be short of friends.

Sun in Gemini with Mercury in Cancer

Alice Bailey	Benazir Bhutto	Jason Donovan
Harry Enfield	Judy Garland	Dorothy L. Sayers

You learn best when you have a warm personal relationship with those who are teaching you. Without this rapport and sense of acceptance, dry, dusty facts and cold, hard logic can be not only uninviting, but also difficult to grasp. Your mind is acutely sensitive to emotional undercurrents and your focus is less on what people are saying than the feelings you sense are being conveyed. Often, after an interchange, you may not be able to remember the exact words that were spoken, but the emotional atmosphere will have made an indelible impression.

Your mind picks up information best through pictures and diagrams, as words alone can go in one ear and out the other, making you seem forgetful, and possibly even a poor learner. In fact, your memory is likely to be exceptionally retentive, once you've formed some kind of emotional relationship with incoming data. You can absorb information almost automatically, like a sponge. Being so intuitive that it verges on the telepathic, you respond instantly to almost invisible clues about how people are feeling, sometimes even when they are at a distance. (The medium Alice Bailey claimed to do this quite literally, channelling information from a disembodied Tibetan master.) This may cloud your judgement, sometimes leading you to say what you think people want to hear, rather than being logical, detached and mentally independent.

Some of your ideas may simply be family prejudices so it's useful to check occasionally whether your opinions are genuinely your own. You can take comments over-personally and be inclined to brood, but can easily snap out of it once you notice yourself doing so. As words, films and poetry are like food to you, it's important that you select your mental diet wisely.

NINE

Venus — At Your Pleasure

♀ THE GLYPH FOR VENUS IS MADE UP OF THE CIRCLE OF ETERNITY on top of the cross of matter. Esoterically this represents love, which is a quality of the divine, revealed on earth through personal choice. The saying 'One man's meat is another man's poison' couldn't be more relevant when it comes to what we love. It is a mystery why we find one thing attractive and another unattractive, or even repulsive. Looking at the sign, aspects and house of your Venus can't give any explanation of this mystery, but it can give some clear indications of what it is that you value and find desirable. This can be quite different from what current fashion tells you you should like. For example, many people are strongly turned on by voluptuous bodies but the media constantly shows images of near-anorexics as the desirable ideal. If you ignore what you, personally, find beautiful and try to be, or to love, what at heart leaves you cold, you are setting yourself up for unnecessary pain and dissatisfaction. Being true to your Venus sign, even if other people think you are strange, brings joy and pleasure. It also builds up your self-esteem because it grounds you solidly in your own personal values. This, in turn, makes you much more attractive to others. Not only that, it improves your relationships immeasurably, because you are living authentically and not betraying yourself by trying to prove your worth to others by being something you are not.

Glittering Venus, the brightest planet in the heavens, was named after the goddess of love, war and victory. Earlier names for her were Aphrodite, Innana and Ishtar. She was beautiful, self-willed and self-indulgent but was also skilled in all the arts of civilisation.

Your Venus sign shows what you desire and would like to possess, not only in relationships but also in all aspects of your taste, from clothes and culture to hobbies and hobby-horses. It identifies how and where you can be charming and seductive and skilful at creating your own type of beauty yourself. It also describes your style of attracting partners and the kind of people that turn you on. When your Venus is activated you feel powerful, desirable and wonderfully, wickedly indulged and indulgent. When it is not, even if someone has all the right credentials to make a good match, the relationship will always lack that certain something. If you don't take the chance to express your Venus to a good enough degree somewhere in your life, you miss out woefully on delight and happiness.

Morning Star, Evening Star

Venus appears in the sky either in the morning or in the evening. The ancients launched their attacks when Venus became a morning star, believing that she was then in her warrior-goddess role, releasing aggressive energy for victory in battle. If you're a morning-star person, you're likely to be impulsive, self-willed and idealistic, prepared to hold out until you find the partner who is just right for you.

Relationships and business dealings of morning-star Venus people are said to prosper best whenever Venus in the sky is a morning star. If you are an early bird, you can check this out. At these times Venus can be seen in the eastern sky before the Sun has risen.

The name for Venus as an evening star is Hesperus and it was then, traditionally, said to be sacred to lovers. Evening-star people tend to be easy-going and are open to negotiation, conciliation and making peace. If you are an evening-star Venus person, your best times in relationship and business affairs are said to be when Venus can be seen, jewel-like, in the western sky after the Sun has set.

Because the orbit of Venus is so close to the Sun, your Venus can only be in one of five signs. You have a morning-star Venus if your Venus is in one of the two signs that come before your Sun sign in the zodiac. You have an evening-star Venus if your Venus is in either of the two signs that follow your Sun sign. If you have Venus in the same sign as your Sun, you could be either, depending on whether your Venus is ahead of or behind your Sun. (You can find out which at the author's website www.janeridderpatrick.com.)

If you don't yet know your Venus sign, you might like to read through all of the following descriptions and see if you can guess what it is. You can find out for sure on pp. 116–18.

At the beginning of each section are the names of some well-known Geminis with that particular Venus sign. You can find out more about them in Chapter Ten, Famous Gemini Birthdays.

Sun in Gemini with Venus in Aries

Helena Bonham Carter	Sir Arthur Conan Doyle	Isadora Duncan
Harry Enfield	Hergé	Marilyn Monroe

At the heart of every drama is a conflict of some kind, and you'll find yourself drawn like a magnet to wherever there is action, either as a major player or as an enthusiastic bystander or commentator – a bit like Hergé's much-loved cartoon character, the reporter and adventure hero Tintin. In relationships you'd like to have the upper hand but will never respect a partner who would let you dominate. When you find someone attractive, you won't hesitate to make the first move and you prefer to be the one in hot pursuit. If you are chased, though, your instinct is to turn tail. With too easy a conquest, you quickly become bored. No challenge means no fun, and the harder to get a person is, the better you like it. You admire feisty, colourful and independent partners who will stand up to you and may even be quite demanding or wilful. Since novels are often partially autobiographical, it's interesting that Conan Doyle's emotionally desiccated creation, Sherlock Holmes, was enthralled by only one woman – a sharp-thinking, courageous and honourable lady who managed to outwit him.

Being outgoing and enthusiastic, with bags of charm and chatter, you can excel in social situations. Understanding and considering other people's feelings, however, doesn't always come easy. If you're in a committed relationship, it's essential that you find some kind of suitable outlet for your restless and dynamic energies. New and challenging projects that you can pour your heart into and then leave behind once they're finished are ideal for you. You love risk, danger and competition, and you'll be sure to find those in your life somewhere.

Sun in Gemini with Venus in Taurus

Paul McCartney	Robert Maxwell	Alison Moyet
Kristin Scott Thomas	Richard Wagner	W.B. Yeats

With Venus in Taurus, there is a powerful desire to hold on to the reins in relationships and to be in control. In fact, there is powerful desire, full stop. You are determined to have whatever it is you desire and hate to let go of what you love, once it is yours. The mystic Irish poet W.B. Yeats kept the flame of unrequited love burning for years for Maud Gonne, a woman who refused him, only marrying years later, when in his 50s, a woman almost 30 years younger than himself. Yet this is in sharp contrast to your Sun in Gemini, which can scarcely bear to sit still in a chair for five minutes at a stretch and is interested in relating to practically everybody, intellectually if not romantically, so you can often find yourself pulled in conflicting directions. What do you want – to have lots of relationships or just one that's stable? With your ability to talk yourself into – and out of – just about anything, like the composer Richard Wagner, who had a devoted wife and a series of love affairs, you might just try to have your cake and eat it too. Beauty, music and colour are vitally important to you, as are solid comfort and the appearance of wealth. Because you enjoy luxury and all the good things in life, your tastes may well be expensive. A home of your own, filled with treasured possessions, can be a stable centre that brings you contentment. Sex, and all the delights of the body, is likely to be a source of enormous pleasure, as it feels so life-affirming for you. You can be attracted to sensual, loyal and dependable partners, preferably with well-lined bank balances.

Gemini Sun with Venus in Gemini

Naomi Campbell	Joan Collins	Jason Donovan
John F. Kennedy	Kylie Minogue	Salman Rushdie

One thing is sure – you do like variety. This doesn't mean that you can't be faithful, but more than likely you are an incorrigible flirt. Whether you mean to follow through on that or not is a matter for speculation. Sexual conquest can matter a great deal less to you than your need to feel free to circulate and talk to whom you like, when you like and for as long as you like. Sex for you is often a means of communication, rather than an expression of love, or even lust. But if it is on offer . . . You may find it hard to be tied down to one particular person and, like J.F.K. and Joan Collins, either have a smorgasbord of love interest or marry several times. To stay happy and true, you need a partner who respects your need for constant stimulation and freedom to party and play.

In love, you like to talk and may even enjoy giving or receiving a running commentary as the bedsprings get a workout. If your partner doesn't give you verbal feedback, you could feel starved and anxious. Sending and receiving witty txt msgs and flirty love letters keeps your heart healthy, as you're attracted to people with good communication skills. You may prefer the light touch in relating, moving on, as if a switch had been thrown, when you start to feel bored. Alternatively, you could be attracted to partners who are chronically unwilling to commit. If this keeps happening to you, you might like to look below the surface at your own fear of commitment. When you do, you're less likely to attract, and be attracted to, those who kiss and run.

Gemini Sun with Venus in Cancer

Maeve Binchy   Cilla Black   Julian Clary
Elizabeth Hurley Jamie Oliver   Lionel Richie

For you, home is where the heart is and your family, or chosen clan of friends, could well form the backbone of your life. The giving and receiving of acceptance and warm emotional support is essential for your happiness and you can even be a little sentimental about shared experiences from the past. Creating a secure, beautiful and comfortable nest where you can retreat from the world is top priority. The prospect of loss of financial security or emotional abandonment can terrify you, yet you may fight against, or deny, your own, or your partner's, dependency. The more honest you are with yourself about how much you need both intimacy and freedom – and find ways of accommodating each of these parts, which are vital for your happiness – the more fulfilled you will be.

You may have a tendency to think you know best what is good for others and could feel miffed if they don't agree. If you're not getting what you want, you could even dabble in a little emotional blackmail, with huffs and blame and sulks, to try to get your way. A big warm cuddle, though, usually sets matters right all round.

You enjoy taking people under your wing and have an acute sense of what people are hungry for and provide it, sometimes literally, like celebrity chef Jamie Oliver. He successfully turned a team of unemployed and untrained young people into top-class chefs who now staff his restaurant. The idea, he said, was to bring out the strengths and weaknesses and personality of each individual. You too have the gift of bringing out the best in people, making them feel cherished and welcome – and that's what you'd love for yourself too.

Gemini Sun with Venus in Leo

Xaviera Hollander Nicole Kidman Malcolm McDowell
Barry Manilow   Charles Saatchi Françoise Sagan

You're a larger-than-life romantic and when you love, you do so whole-heartedly. You'll throw yourself into relationships with passion and commitment. You need a partner you can be proud of and whose glamour and cachet enhance your own sense of glory and importance. With your love of the theatrical and strong desire to impress, you may attract, and be attracted to, flamboyant partners – or be one yourself. Controversial art collector and advertising executive Charles Saatchi's romance with cookery diva Nigella Lawson is a case in point. Some with this placement, whose hearts haven't been touched, aren't averse to using others to advance their careers or social standing.

You need to know that you're appreciated and respected, and can't bear to be overlooked or seen as less than special. As your pride's easily hurt, you need a lot of reassurance and fussing over – and sometimes trowel-loads of flattery – to be convinced that you really are loved. Slighting you or treating you casually are the quickest ways to drive you into the arms of someone more appreciative, even though, by inclination, you're naturally faithful. In your book, infidelity and disloyalty are hanging offences. You believe totally in your projects, romantic or otherwise, but as you identify with them so closely, you may tend to see others as extensions of yourself and feel offended when they refuse to submit to your well-meaning bossiness. Shifting gear from the high-voltage drama of romantic love to confront the humdrum realities of everyday life that come with a long-term, committed relationship may be a tough challenge for you. A lively social calendar and finding ways of infusing pomp and circumstance into partnerships will keep love blossoming and boredom at bay.

TEN

Famous Gemini Birthdays

FIND OUT WHO SHARES YOUR MOON, MERCURY AND VENUS SIGNS, and any challenging Sun aspects, and see what they have done with the material they were born with. Notice how often it is not just the personalities of the people themselves but the roles of actors, characters of authors and works of artists that reflect their astrological make-up. In reading standard biographies, I've been constantly astounded – and, of course, delighted – at how often phrases used to describe individuals could have been lifted straight from their astrological profiles. Check it out yourself!

A few people below have been given a choice of two Moons. This is because the Moon changed sign on the day that they were born and no birth time was available. You may be able to guess which one is correct if you read the descriptions of the Moon signs in Chapter Seven.

21 May

1916 Harold Robbins, American bestselling novelist, *The Carpetbaggers*
Sun aspects: none
Moon: Capricorn/Aquarius   Mercury: Gemini
Venus: Cancer

22 May

1859 Sir Arthur Conan Doyle, Scottish writer and creator of Sherlock Holmes
Sun aspects: Uranus
Moon: Aquarius   Mercury: Taurus   Venus: Aries

23 May

1734 Franz Anton Mesmer, founder of mesmerism (hypnotism)
Sun aspects: none
Moon: Aquarius   Mercury: Taurus   Venus: Aries

24 May

1960 Kristin Scott Thomas, actress, *The English Patient* and *Gosford Park*
Sun aspects: Pluto
Moon: Taurus   Mercury: Gemini   Venus: Taurus

25 May

1887 Padre Pio, Italian saint gifted with the ability to appear in two places at once
Sun aspects: Neptune, Pluto
Moon: Cancer   Mercury: Gemini   Venus: Cancer

26 May

1907 John Wayne, cowboy film actor, *True Grit* and *The Shootist*
Sun aspects: none
Moon: Scorpio   Mercury: Gemini   Venus: Taurus

27 May
1877 Isadora Duncan, controversial dancer who died when her scarf caught in the wheel of her car
Sun aspects: none
Moon: Aries   Mercury: Taurus   Venus: Aries

28 May
1908 Ian Fleming, creator of James Bond
Sun aspects: none
Moon: Taurus   Mercury: Gemini   Venus: Cancer

29 May
1917 John F. Kennedy, charismatic US President assassinated in 1963
Sun aspects: none
Moon: Virgo   Mercury: Taurus   Venus: Gemini

30 May
1961 Harry Enfield, comedian
Sun aspects: Pluto
Moon: Sagittarius   Mercury: Cancer   Venus: Aries

31 May
1819 Walt Whitman, American poet, *Leaves of Grass*
Sun aspects: none
Moon: Leo/Virgo   Mercury: Taurus   Venus: Taurus

1 June
1926 Marilyn Monroe, screen goddess, *Some Like it Hot*, *The Seven Year Itch*
Sun aspects: none
Moon: Aquarius   Mercury: Gemini   Venus: Aries

2 June
1840 Thomas Hardy, English novelist, *Far from the Madding Crowd*
Sun aspects: Saturn, Uranus
Moon: Cancer   Mercury: Gemini   Venus: Taurus

3 June
1906 Josephine Baker, cosmopolitan black American entertainer
Sun aspects: Saturn, Pluto
Moon: Libra   Mercury: Gemini   Venus: Cancer

4 June
1907 Patience Strong, writer of inspirational verse
Sun aspects: none
Moon: Pisces   Mercury: Gemini   Venus: Taurus

5 June
1883 John Maynard Keynes, creator of the World Bank and the International Monetary Fund (IMF)
Sun aspects: Uranus
Moon: Gemini   Mercury: Gemini   Venus: Taurus

6 June
1875 Thomas Mann, author, *Buddenbrooks* and *Death in Venice*
Sun aspects: none
Moon: Cancer   Mercury: Cancer   Venus: Taurus

7 June

1848 Paul Gauguin, French painter who left Paris to live on a Pacific island
Sun aspects: Saturn
Moon: Virgo   Mercury: Cancer   Venus: Gemini

8 June

1867 Frank Lloyd Wright, innovative architect and pioneer of open-plan design
Sun aspects: none
Moon: Virgo   Mercury: Gemini   Venus: Taurus

9 June

1781 George Stephenson, English engineer and 'father of the railways'
Sun aspects: Saturn, Uranus
Moon: Capricorn/Aquarius   Mercury: Gemini
Venus: Gemini

10 June

1966 Elizabeth Hurley, model and actress
Sun aspects: Saturn, Uranus, Pluto
Moon: Scorpio   Mercury: Gemini   Venus: Cancer

11 June

1910 Jacques Cousteau, underwater explorer and photographer
Sun aspects: Pluto
Moon: Leo   Mercury: Taurus   Venus: Taurus

12 June
1929 Anne Frank, Jewish girl whose diary recorded Nazi persecution
Sun aspects: Saturn
Moon: Leo   Mercury: Gemini   Venus: Taurus

13 June
1893 Dorothy L. Sayers, mystery writer and creator of Lord Peter Wimsey
Sun aspects: none
Moon: Gemini   Mercury: Cancer   Venus: Cancer

14 June
1811 Harriet Beecher Stowe, author and abolitionist, *Uncle Tom's Cabin*
Sun aspects: Saturn, Pluto
Moon: Aries   Mercury: Gemini   Venus: Taurus

15 June
1964 Courteney Cox, actress who plays the uptight Monica in *Friends*
Sun aspects: none
Moon: Virgo   Mercury: Gemini   Venus: Cancer

16 June
1880 Alice Bailey, esoteric writer and medium
Sun aspects: none
Moon: Libra   Mercury: Cancer   Venus: Gemini

17 June
1898 M.C. Escher, artist of mind-teasing works of optical illusion
Sun aspects: Neptune
Moon: Gemini   Mercury: Gemini   Venus: Cancer

18 June
1942 Paul McCartney, musician and member of The Beatles
Sun aspects: Neptune
Moon: Leo   Mercury: Gemini   Venus: Taurus

19 June
1896 Wallis Simpson, American divorcee whom King
Edward VIII abdicated to marry
Sun aspects: none
Moon: Libra   Mercury: Gemini   Venus: Gemini

20 June
1967 Nicole Kidman, actress, *Portrait of a Lady*, *Moulin
Rouge*
Sun aspects: Uranus
Moon: Sagittarius   Mercury: Cancer   Venus: Leo

21 June
1935 Françoise Sagan, French author, *Bonjour Tristesse*, *A
Certain Smile*
Sun aspects: none
Moon: Pisces   Mercury: Gemini   Venus: Leo

Other Gemini people mentioned in this book
Patch Adams, unconventional doctor and clown ☆ Stanley Baxter,
Scottish comedian and impersonator ☆ Lord Beaverbrook,
newspaper magnate, *The Daily Express* ☆ Benazir Bhutto, former
female Prime Minister of Pakistan ☆ Maeve Binchy, author, *Tara
Road*, *Circle Of Friends* ☆ Cilla Black, singer and TV personality,
Blind Date ☆ Helena Bonham Carter, actress, *Howards End* ☆ Björn
Borg, tennis champion and ladies' man ☆ Kathy Burke,
comedian, *Gimme Gimme Gimme* ☆ Barbara Bush, wife and mother
of American presidents George and George W. Bush ☆ Simon

Callow, actor, *Four Weddings and a Funeral* ☆ Alastair Campbell, Tony Blair's former press secretary and spin doctor ☆ Naomi Campbell, supermodel ☆ Rachel Carson, environmentalist writer, *Silent Spring* ☆ Charles II, King of Scotland and England and father of many illegitimate offspring ☆ G.K. Chesterton, crime writer, creator of *Father Brown* ☆ Julian Clary, comedian 'more camp than a row of tents' ☆ Joan Collins, actress, *Dynasty* ☆ Tony Curtis, actor, *The Boston Strangler* ☆ Jeffrey Dahmer, serial killer of homosexual men, whom he dismembered and ate ☆ Johnny Depp, actor, *Edward Scissorhands* ☆ Richard Dimbleby, TV presenter and reverential commentator on 1950s state occasions ☆ Margaret Drabble, author, *Safe as Houses* ☆ Jason Donovan, actor, *Neighbours* ☆ Bob Dylan, singer and songwriter, 'Blowin' in the Wind' ☆ Edward Elgar, composer, *Pomp and Circumstance* ☆ Salvatore Ferragamo, upmarket shoemaker ☆ Judy Garland, actress, *The Wizard of Oz* ☆ Boy George, singer, 'Do You Really Want to Hurt Me' ☆ Allen Ginsberg, American poet of the Beat Generation ☆ Rudolph Giuliani, former Mayor of New York ☆ Katharine Graham, proprietor of the *New York Post* newspaper which exposed the Watergate cover-up ☆ Earl Haig, soldier and activist on behalf of wounded and unemployed ex-servicemen ☆ Gilbert Harding, irascible radio and TV personality in the 1950s, *The Brains Trust* ☆ Hergé, Belgian cartoonist and creator of Tintin ☆ Xaviera Hollander, internationally notorious brothel-owner and writer of *The Happy Hooker* ☆ Tom Jones, singer, 'It's Not Unusual' ☆ Henry Kissinger, US Secretary of State, diplomat and Nobel Peace Prize winner ☆ Peggy Lee, singer and songwriter, 'I'm a Woman' ☆ Colleen McCullough, author, *The Thorn Birds* ☆ Malcolm McDowell, actor, *A Clockwork Orange* ☆ Barry Manilow, singer, 'Copacabana' ☆ Dean Martin, singer and actor, 'When You're Smiling' ☆ Robert Maxwell, media mogul who defrauded millions from employees' pension funds ☆ Kylie Minogue, actress and singer, *Neighbours* ☆ Alanis Morissette, singer, *Jagged Little Pill* ☆ Alison Moyet, singer, 'All Cried Out' ☆ Liam Neeson, actor, *Schindler's List* ☆ Jamie Oliver, TV celebrity chef ☆ Norman Vincent Peale, inspirational writer, *The Tough-Minded Optimist* ☆ Prince Philip, consort to Queen Elizabeth II ☆ Alexander Pope, satirical poet, *The Rape of the Lock* ☆ Enoch Powell, right-wing politician opposed to immigration ☆ Priscilla Presley, actress and wife of Elvis, *Dallas* ☆ Lionel Richie, singer, 'Hello', 'Three Times a Lady' ☆ Isabella Rossellini, actress, *Blue Velvet* ☆ Salman Rushdie, author who received death threats from Islamic fundamentalists for his *Satanic Verses* ☆ Charles Saatchi, controversial art collector ☆ Jean-Paul Sartre, existentialist writer, *Being and Nothingness* ☆ Brooke Shields, actress, *Pretty Baby* ☆ Nancy Sinatra, singer, 'These Boots Are Made for Walking' ☆ Delia Smith, celebrity TV cook and writer ☆ Jackie Stewart, racing driver ☆ Donald Trump, flamboyant US property developer with a taste for grandiose buildings ☆ Richard Wagner, opera composer, *Tristan und Isolde* ☆ Mary Whitehouse, campaigner against sex, violence and blasphemy on TV ☆ Venus Williams, tennis champion ☆ W.B. Yeats, Irish poet, *The Tower* ☆ Brigham Young, American Mormon leader who died in 1877 leaving $2.5 million, 17 wives and 56 children.

ELEVEN

Finding Your Sun, Moon, Mercury and Venus Signs

ALL OF THE ASTROLOGICAL DATA IN THIS BOOK WAS CALCULATED by Astrolabe, who also supply a wide range of astrological software. I am most grateful for their help and generosity.

ASTROLABE, PO Box 1750, Brewster, MA 02631, USA www.alabe.com

PLEASE NOTE THAT ALL OF THE TIMES GIVEN ARE IN GREENWICH MEAN TIME (GMT). If you were born during British Summer Time (BST) you will need to subtract one hour from your birth time to convert it to GMT. If you were born outside of the British Isles, find the time zone of your place of birth and the number of hours it is different from GMT. Add the difference in hours if you were born west of the UK, and subtract the difference if you were born east of the UK to convert your birth time to GMT.

Your Sun Sign

Check your year of birth, and if you were born between the dates and times given the Sun was in Gemini when you were born – confirming that you're a Gemini. If you were born before the time on the date that Gemini begins in your year, you are a Taurean. If you were born after the time on the date Gemini ends in your year, you are a Cancerian.

Your Moon Sign

The Moon changes sign every two and a half days. To find your Moon sign, first find your year of birth. You will notice that in each year box there are three columns.

The second column shows the day of the month that the Moon changed sign, while the first column gives the abbreviation for the sign that the Moon entered on that date.

In the middle column, the month has been omitted, so that the dates run from, for example, 20 to 31 (May) and then from 1 to 21 (June).

In the third column, after the star, the time that the Moon changed sign on that day is given.

Look down the middle column of your year box to find your date of birth. If your birth date is given, look to the third column to find the time that the Moon changed sign. If you were born after that time, your Moon sign is given in the first column next to your birth date. If you were born before that time, your Moon sign is the one above the one next to your birth date.

If your birth date is not given, find the closest date before it. The sign shown next to that date is your Moon sign.

If you were born on a day that the Moon changed signs and you do not know your time of birth, try out both of that day's Moon signs and feel which one fits you best.

The abbreviations for the signs are as follows:

Aries – Ari   Taurus – Tau   Gemini – Gem   Cancer – Can
Leo – Leo   Virgo – Vir   Libra – Lib   Scorpio – Sco
Sagittarius – Sag   Capricorn – Cap   Aquarius – Aqu   Pisces – Pis

Your Mercury Sign

Find your year of birth and then the column in which your birthday falls. Look up to the top of the column to find your Mercury sign. You will see that some dates appear twice. This is because Mercury changed sign that day. If your birthday falls on one of these dates, try out both Mercury signs and see which one fits you best. If you know your birth time, you can find out for sure which Mercury sign is yours on my website – www.janeridderpatrick.com.

Your Venus Sign

Find your year of birth and then the column in which your birthday falls. Look up to the top of the column to find your Venus sign. Some dates have two possible signs. That's because Venus changed signs that day. Try them both out and see which fits you best. If the year you are interested in doesn't appear in the tables, or you have Venus in the same sign as your Sun and want to know whether you have a morning or evening star Venus, you can find the information on my website – www.janeridderpatrick.com.

♊ Gemini Sun Tables ☉

YEAR	GEMINI BEGINS	GEMINI ENDS
1930	21 May 19.42	22 Jun 03.52
1931	22 May 01.15	22 Jun 09.28
1932	21 May 07.06	21 Jun 15.22
1933	21 May 12.56	21 Jun 21.11
1934	21 May 18.35	22 Jun 02.47
1935	22 May 00.24	22 Jun 08.37
1936	21 May 06.07	21 Jun 14.21
1937	21 May 11.57	21 Jun 20.12
1938	21 May 17.50	22 Jun 02.02
1939	21 May 23.26	22 Jun 07.39
1940	21 May 05.23	21 Jun 13.36
1941	21 May 11.22	21 Jun 19.33
1942	21 May 17.08	22 Jun 01.16
1943	21 May 23.02	22 Jun 07.12
1944	21 May 04.50	21 Jun 13.02
1945	21 May 10.40	21 Jun 18.52
1946	21 May 16.33	22 Jun 00.44
1947	21 May 22.09	22 Jun 06.18
1948	21 May 03.57	21 Jun 12.10
1949	21 May 09.50	21 Jun 18.02
1950	21 May 15.27	21 Jun 23.36
1951	21 May 21.15	22 Jun 05.24
1952	21 May 03.03	21 Jun 11.12
1953	21 May 08.52	21 Jun 16.59
1954	21 May 14.47	21 Jun 16.59
1955	21 May 20.24	22 Jun 04.31
1956	21 May 02.12	21 Jun10.23
1957	21 May 08.10	21 Jun 16.20
1958	21 May 13.51	21 Jun 21.56
1959	21 May 19.42	22 Jun 03.49
1960	21 May 01.33	21 Jun 09.42
1961	21 May 07.22	21 Jun 15.30
1962	21 May 13.16	21 Jun 21.24
1963	21 May 18.58	22 Jun 03.04

YEAR	GEMINI	CANCER
1964	21 May 00.49	21 Jun 08.56
1965	21 May 06.50	21 Jun 14.55
1966	21 May 12.32	21 Jun 20.33
1967	21 May 18.17	22 Jun 02.22
1968	21 May 00.05	21 Jun 08.13
1969	21 May 05.49	21 Jun 13.55
1970	21 May 11.37	21 Jun 19.42
1971	21 May 17.15	22 Jun 01.19
1972	20 May 22.59	21 Jun 07.06
1973	21 May 04.53	21 Jun 13.00
1974	21 May 10.36	21 Jun 18.37
1975	21 May 16.23	22 Jun 00.26
1976	20 May 22.21	21 Jun 06.24
1977	21 May 04.14	21 Jun 12.13
1978	21 May 10.08	21 Jun 18.09
1979	21 May 15.53	21 Jun 23.56
1980	20 May 21.42	21 Jun 05.47
1981	21 May 03.39	21 Jun 11.44
1982	21 May 09.22	21 Jun 17.23
1983	21 May 15.06	21 Jun 23.08
1984	20 May 20.57	21 Jun 05.02
1985	21 May 02.42	21 Jun 10.55
1986	21 May 08.27	21 Jun 16.29
1987	21 May 14.10	21 Jun 22.10
1988	20 May 19.56	21 Jun 03.56
1989	21 May 01.53	21 Jun 09.53
1990	21 May 07.37	21 Jun 15.32
1991	21 May 13.20	21 Jun 21.18
1992	20 May 19.12	21 Jun 03.14
1993	21 May 01.01	21 Jun 08.59
1994	21 May 06.48	21 Jun 14.47
1995	21 May 12.34	21 Jun 20.34
1996	20 May 18.23	21 Jun 02.23
1997	21 May 00.17	21 Jun 08.19
1998	21 May 06.05	21 Jun 14.02
1999	21 May 11.52	21 Jun 19.49
2000	20 May 17.49	21 Jun 01.47

♊ Gemini – Finding Your Moon Sign ☽

1930		
Ari	23	*05:55
Tau	25	*14:14
Gem	27	*19:06
Can	29	*21:25
Leo	31	*22:45
Vir	3	*00:37
Lib	5	*04:04
Sco	7	*09:30
Sag	9	*16:56
Cap	12	*02:20
Aqu	14	*13:39
Pis	17	*02:11
Ari	19	*14:14
Tau	21	*23:33

1931		
Leo	22	*11:26
Vir	24	*15:06
Lib	26	*17:50
Sco	28	*20:07
Sag	30	*22:48
Cap	2	*03:08
Aqu	4	*10:24
Pis	6	*21:01
Ari	9	*09:43
Tau	11	*21:53
Gem	14	*07:21
Can	16	*13:37
Leo	18	*17:36
Vir	20	*20:32

1932		
Cap	22	*07:12
Aqu	24	*10:32
Pis	26	*17:57
Ari	29	*05:08
Tau	31	*18:04
Gem	3	*06:32
Can	5	*17:20
Leo	8	*02:13
Vir	10	*09:05
Lib	12	*13:40
Sco	14	*15:59
Sag	16	*16:45
Cap	18	*17:31
Aqu	20	*20:12

1933		
Tau	21	*16:26
Gem	24	*04:31
Can	26	*17:11
Leo	29	*05:33
Vir	31	*16:05
Lib	2	*23:13
Sco	5	*02:23
Sag	7	*02:31
Cap	9	*01:33
Aqu	11	*01:42
Pis	13	*04:50
Ari	15	*11:51
Tau	17	*22:12
Gem	20	*10:25

1934		
Vir	21	*15:34
Lib	24	*01:41
Sco	26	*07:51
Sag	28	*10:27
Cap	30	*11:11
Aqu	1	*11:55
Pis	3	*14:07
Ari	5	*18:31
Tau	8	*01:17
Gem	10	*10:14
Can	12	*21:14
Leo	15	*09:52
Vir	17	*22:50
Lib	20	*09:57

♊ Gemini – Finding Your Moon Sign ☽

1935			1936			1937			1938			1939		
Aqu	23	*01:08	Can	22	*23:20	Sco	22	*11:18	Pis	22	*11:07	Can	21	*12:22
Pis	25	*04:13	Leo	25	*04:41	Sag	25	*00:09	Ari	24	*19:34	Leo	23	*14:33
Ari	27	*06:58	Vir	27	*13:48	Cap	27	*12:52	Tau	27	*00:15	Vir	25	*16:50
Tau	29	*09:59	Lib	30	*01:38	Aqu	30	*00:12	Gem	29	*01:51	Lib	27	*20:06
Gem	31	*14:11	Sco	1	*14:10	Pis	1	*08:56	Can	31	*01:52	Sco	30	*00:47
Can	2	*20:44	Sag	4	*01:36	Ari	3	*14:20	Leo	2	*02:09	Sag	1	*07:15
Leo	5	*06:19	Cap	6	*11:01	Tau	5	*16:35	Vir	4	*04:21	Cap	3	*15:50
Vir	7	*18:25	Aqu	8	*18:17	Gem	7	*16:45	Lib	6	*09:36	Aqu	6	*02:40
Lib	10	*06:59	Pis	10	*23:26	Can	9	*16:31	Sco	8	*18:01	Pis	8	*15:04
Sco	12	*17:35	Ari	13	*02:46	Leo	11	*17:44	Sag	11	*04:57	Ari	11	*03:09
Sag	15	*00:55	Tau	15	*04:48	Vir	13	*22:02	Cap	13	*17:20	Tau	13	*12:41
Cap	17	*05:20	Gem	17	*06:29	Lib	16	*06:08	Aqu	16	*06:07	Gem	15	*18:31
Aqu	19	*07:55	Can	19	*09:09	Sco	18	*17:30	Pis	18	*18:02	Can	17	*21:05
Pis	21	*09:55	Leo	21	*14:06	Sag	21	*06:25	Ari	21	*03:38	Leo	19	*21:57
												Vir	21	*22:56

♊ Gemini – Finding Your Moon Sign ☽

1940		
Sag	21	*13:00
Cap	23	*16:35
Aqu	25	*23:20
Pis	28	*09:39
Ari	30	*22:18
Tau	2	*10:42
Gem	4	*20:48
Can	7	*04:01
Leo	9	*09:00
Vir	11	*12:40
Lib	13	*15:43
Sco	15	*18:31
Sag	17	*21:34
Cap	20	*01:45

1941		
Tau	23	*07:26
Gem	25	*20:09
Can	28	*07:36
Leo	30	*17:14
Vir	2	*00:37
Lib	4	*05:16
Sco	6	*07:13
Sag	8	*07:23
Cap	10	*07:31
Aqu	12	*09:42
Pis	14	*15:34
Ari	17	*01:30
Tau	19	*14:02

1942		
Vir	23	*06:07
Lib	25	*13:20
Sco	27	*16:31
Sag	29	*16:38
Cap	31	*15:43
Aqu	2	*15:59
Pis	4	*19:14
Ari	7	*02:11
Tau	9	*12:16
Gem	12	*00:11
Can	14	*12:49
Leo	17	*01:18
Vir	19	*12:32
Lib	21	*21:03

1943		
Cap	22	*01:59
Aqu	24	*03:23
Pis	26	*05:57
Ari	28	*10:16
Tau	30	*16:25
Gem	2	*00:30
Can	4	*10:45
Leo	6	*23:03
Vir	9	*12:02
Lib	11	*23:20
Sco	14	*06:58
Sag	16	*10:34
Cap	18	*11:29
Aqu	20	*11:33

1944		
Gem	22	*04:26
Can	24	*10:04
Leo	26	*19:04
Vir	29	*06:58
Lib	31	*19:37
Sco	3	*06:31
Sag	5	*14:26
Cap	7	*19:40
Aqu	9	*23:11
Pis	12	*01:58
Ari	14	*04:40
Tau	16	*07:51
Gem	18	*12:11
Can	20	*18:28

Ⅱ Gemini – Finding Your Moon Sign ☽

1945

Lib	21	*14:43
Sco	24	*03:20
Sag	26	*15:10
Cap	29	*01:23
Aqu	31	*09:34
Pis	2	*15:24
Ari	4	*18:50
Tau	6	*20:22
Gem	8	*21:14
Can	10	*23:02
Leo	13	*03:20
Vir	15	*11:08
Lib	17	*22:06
Sco	20	*10:35

1946

Aqu	21	*14:30
Pis	23	*23:37
Ari	26	*05:04
Tau	28	*07:03
Gem	30	*06:54
Can	1	*06:28
Leo	3	*07:39
Vir	5	*11:58
Lib	7	*19:57
Sco	10	*07:04
Sag	12	*19:50
Cap	15	*08:39
Aqu	17	*20:15
Pis	20	*05:42

1947

Can	22	*16:26
Leo	24	*17:18
Vir	26	*19:50
Lib	29	*00:54
Sco	31	*08:42
Sag	2	*18:54
Cap	5	*06:51
Aqu	7	*19:37
Pis	10	*07:46
Ari	12	*17:33
Tau	14	*23:43
Gem	17	*02:20
Can	19	*02:31

1948

Sag	22	*21:22
Cap	25	*05:07
Aqu	27	*15:31
Pis	30	*03:45
Ari	1	*15:54
Tau	4	*01:42
Gem	6	*08:05
Can	8	*11:27
Leo	10	*13:11
Vir	12	*14:48
Lib	14	*17:33
Sco	16	*22:03
Sag	19	*04:28
Cap	21	*12:51

1949

Ari	22	*11:01
Tau	24	*23:40
Gem	27	*10:26
Can	29	*18:38
Leo	1	*00:35
Vir	3	*04:53
Lib	5	*07:57
Sco	7	*10:13
Sag	9	*12:23
Cap	11	*15:40
Aqu	13	*21:27
Pis	16	*06:38
Ari	18	*18:44
Tau	21	*07:29

♊ Gemini – Finding Your Moon Sign ☽

1950		
Leo	22	*08:05
Vir	24	*15:49
Lib	26	*20:25
Sco	28	*22:00
Sag	30	*21:43
Cap	1	*21:27
Aqu	3	*23:19
Pis	6	*04:57
Ari	8	*14:44
Tau	11	*03:12
Gem	13	*16:04
Can	16	*03:44
Leo	18	*13:36
Vir	20	*21:30

1951		
Sag	21	*06:43
Cap	23	*06:06
Aqu	25	*06:41
Pis	27	*10:06
Ari	29	*16:53
Tau	1	*02:33
Gem	3	*14:02
Can	6	*02:31
Leo	8	*15:11
Vir	11	*02:45
Lib	13	*11:29
Sco	15	*16:16
Sag	17	*17:25
Cap	19	*16:37
Aqu	21	*16:04

1952		
Tau	21	*07:29
Gem	23	*14:37
Can	26	*00:06
Leo	28	*11:59
Vir	31	*00:56
Lib	2	*12:24
Sco	4	*20:18
Sag	7	*00:19
Cap	9	*01:45
Aqu	11	*02:26
Pis	13	*04:00
Ari	15	*07:29
Tau	17	*13:11
Gem	19	*21:03

1953		
Lib	23	*08:15
Sco	25	*19:31
Sag	28	*04:07
Cap	30	*10:16
Aqu	1	*14:44
Pis	3	*18:11
Ari	5	*21:01
Tau	7	*23:41
Gem	10	*03:03
Can	12	*08:17
Leo	14	*16:27
Vir	17	*03:36
Lib	19	*16:16

1954		
Aqu	23	*00:47
Pis	25	*07:07
Ari	27	*10:30
Tau	29	*11:32
Gem	31	*11:40
Can	2	*12:46
Leo	4	*16:34
Vir	7	*00:07
Lib	9	*10:59
Sco	11	*23:29
Sag	14	*11:36
Cap	16	*22:04
Aqu	19	*06:25
Pis	21	*12:35

♊ Gemini – Finding Your Moon Sign ☽

1955		
Gem	21	*20:56
Can	23	*20:33
Leo	25	*21:53
Vir	28	*02:16
Lib	30	*10:08
Sco	1	*20:54
Sag	4	*09:23
Cap	6	*22:20
Aqu	9	*10:29
Pis	11	*20:31
Ari	14	*03:22
Tau	16	*06:49
Gem	18	*07:36
Can	20	*07:15

1956		
Sco	21	*23:27
Sag	24	*08:46
Cap	26	*20:11
Aqu	29	*08:51
Pis	31	*21:08
Ari	3	*07:04
Tau	5	*13:20
Gem	7	*16:08
Can	9	*16:41
Leo	11	*16:44
Vir	13	*18:03
Lib	15	*21:59
Sco	18	*05:02
Sag	20	*14:55

1957		
Pis	21	*16:20
Ari	24	*04:33
Tau	26	*14:42
Gem	28	*21:45
Can	31	*02:04
Leo	2	*04:44
Vir	4	*06:59
Lib	6	*09:45
Sco	8	*13:41
Sag	10	*19:09
Cap	13	*02:36
Aqu	15	*12:23
Pis	18	*00:14
Ari	20	*12:45

1958		
Can	21	*09:22
Leo	23	*16:14
Vir	25	*20:59
Lib	27	*23:54
Sco	30	*01:33
Sag	1	*02:53
Cap	3	*05:22
Aqu	5	*10:34
Pis	7	*19:24
Ari	10	*07:20
Tau	12	*20:12
Gem	15	*07:30
Can	17	*16:03
Leo	19	*22:03

1959		
Sag	22	*11:50
Cap	24	*11:24
Aqu	26	*13:10
Pis	28	*18:42
Ari	31	*04:18
Tau	2	*16:36
Gem	5	*05:35
Can	7	*17:43
Leo	10	*04:18
Vir	12	*12:49
Lib	14	*18:41
Sco	16	*21:37
Sag	18	*22:14
Cap	20	*22:01

♊ Gemini – Finding Your Moon Sign ☽

1960		
Tau	22	*17:00
Gem	25	*03:54
Can	27	*16:06
Leo	30	*04:50
Vir	1	*16:37
Lib	4	*01:29
Sco	6	*06:19
Sag	8	*07:30
Cap	10	*06:47
Aqu	12	*06:22
Pis	14	*08:18
Ari	16	*13:43
Tau	18	*22:33
Gem	21	*09:46

1961		
Vir	22	*13:37
Lib	25	*01:16
Sco	27	*09:33
Sag	29	*14:09
Cap	31	*16:19
Aqu	2	*17:44
Pis	4	*19:50
Ari	6	*23:24
Tau	9	*04:37
Gem	11	*11:40
Can	13	*20:50
Leo	16	*08:15
Vir	18	*21:11
Lib	21	*09:30

1962		
Cap	22	*01:07
Aqu	24	*06:30
Pis	26	*10:28
Ari	28	*13:14
Tau	30	*15:16
Gem	1	*17:40
Can	3	*21:57
Leo	6	*05:23
Vir	8	*16:12
Lib	11	*04:50
Sco	13	*16:44
Sag	16	*02:02
Cap	18	*08:29
Aqu	20	*12:48

1963		
Tau	21	*02:20
Gem	23	*01:53
Can	25	*02:29
Leo	27	*05:58
Vir	29	*13:22
Lib	1	*00:09
Sco	3	*12:38
Sag	6	*01:00
Cap	8	*12:06
Aqu	10	*21:21
Pis	13	*04:20
Ari	15	*08:45
Tau	17	*10:53
Gem	19	*11:43
Can	21	*12:47

1964		
Lib	21	*00:42
Sco	23	*10:58
Sag	25	*23:03
Cap	28	*11:59
Aqu	31	*00:31
Pis	2	*11:00
Ari	4	*18:02
Tau	6	*21:18
Gem	8	*21:49
Can	10	*21:16
Leo	12	*21:35
Vir	15	*00:28
Lib	17	*06:54
Sco	19	*16:49

♊ Gemini – Finding Your Moon Sign ☽

1965		
Pis	23	*10:13
Ari	25	*20:17
Tau	28	*02:47
Gem	30	*05:58
Can	1	*07:05
Leo	3	*07:46
Vir	5	*09:33
Lib	7	*13:30
Sco	9	*20:04
Sag	12	*05:09
Cap	14	*16:20
Aqu	17	*04:51
Pis	19	*17:28

1966		
Can	22	*16:59
Leo	24	*20:36
Vir	26	*23:21
Lib	29	*02:00
Sco	31	*05:11
Sag	2	*09:39
Cap	4	*16:10
Aqu	7	*01:21
Pis	9	*12:57
Ari	12	*01:25
Tau	14	*12:28
Gem	16	*20:25
Can	19	*01:04
Leo	21	*03:28

1967		
Sco	21	*16:29
Sag	23	*17:05
Cap	25	*18:58
Aqu	27	*23:45
Pis	30	*08:18
Ari	1	*20:06
Tau	4	*09:03
Gem	6	*20:51
Can	9	*06:17
Leo	11	*13:18
Vir	13	*18:23
Lib	15	*21:57
Sco	18	*00:24
Sag	20	*02:19

1968		
Ari	21	*18:14
Tau	24	*06:15
Gem	26	*19:11
Can	29	*07:42
Leo	31	*18:53
Vir	3	*03:51
Lib	5	*09:48
Sco	7	*12:29
Sag	9	*12:41
Cap	11	*12:05
Aqu	13	*12:47
Pis	15	*16:42
Ari	18	*00:50
Tau	20	*12:25

1969		
Leo	21	*18:12
Vir	24	*06:06
Lib	26	*15:06
Sco	28	*20:04
Sag	30	*21:29
Cap	1	*21:06
Aqu	3	*21:04
Pis	5	*23:14
Ari	8	*04:36
Tau	10	*13:06
Gem	12	*23:48
Can	15	*11:52
Leo	18	*00:35
Vir	20	*12:52

♊ Gemini – Finding Your Moon Sign ☽

1970			1971			1972			1973			1974		
Sag	21	*04:10	Tau	22	*06:31	Lib	22	*13:36	Aqu	22	*14:16	Gem	21	*19:53
Cap	23	*07:12	Gem	24	*08:01	Sco	25	*02:00	Pis	25	*01:03	Can	23	*21:45
Aqu	25	*09:25	Can	26	*11:27	Sag	27	*14:32	Ari	27	*08:13	Leo	25	*23:12
Pis	27	*11:58	Leo	28	*18:16	Cap	30	*02:12	Tau	29	*11:26	Vir	28	*01:26
Ari	29	*15:26	Vir	31	*04:48	Aqu	1	*12:14	Gem	31	*11:52	Lib	30	*05:15
Tau	31	*20:03	Lib	2	*17:26	Pis	3	*19:51	Can	2	*11:21	Sco	1	*11:11
Gem	3	*02:10	Sco	5	*05:35	Ari	6	*00:26	Leo	4	*11:50	Sag	3	*19:21
Can	5	*10:26	Sag	7	*15:27	Tau	8	*02:13	Vir	6	*14:52	Cap	6	*05:48
Leo	7	*21:17	Cap	9	*22:44	Gem	10	*02:24	Lib	8	*21:16	Aqu	8	*18:01
Vir	10	*10:01	Aqu	12	*04:02	Can	12	*02:45	Sco	11	*06:51	Pis	11	*06:43
Lib	12	*22:26	Pis	14	*08:01	Leo	14	*05:09	Sag	13	*18:42	Ari	13	*17:52
Sco	15	*08:00	Ari	16	*11:05	Vir	16	*11:04	Cap	16	*07:36	Tau	16	*01:45
Sag	17	*13:37	Tau	18	*13:38	Lib	18	*20:39				Gem	18	*05:58
Cap	19	*16:04	Gem	20	*16:23	Sco	21	*08:42				Can	20	*07:20
Aqu	21	*17:00												

♊ Gemini – Finding Your Moon Sign ☽

1975

Sco	22	*20:25
Sag	24	*23:52
Cap	27	*05:30
Aqu	29	*14:10
Pis	1	*01:32
Ari	3	*14:00
Tau	6	*01:17
Gem	8	*09:48
Can	10	*15:20
Leo	12	*18:45
Vir	14	*21:10
Lib	16	*23:41
Sco	19	*02:59
Sag	21	*07:34

1976

Ari	23	*09:07
Tau	25	*22:06
Gem	28	*10:21
Can	30	*20:38
Leo	2	*04:37
Vir	4	*10:20
Lib	6	*13:59
Sco	8	*15:57
Sag	10	*17:06
Cap	12	*18:45
Aqu	14	*22:32
Pis	17	*05:43
Ari	19	*16:32

1977

Leo	23	*09:12
Vir	25	*18:30
Lib	28	*00:26
Sco	30	*02:55
Sag	1	*02:53
Cap	3	*02:07
Aqu	5	*02:44
Pis	7	*06:35
Ari	9	*14:35
Tau	12	*01:56
Gem	14	*14:49
Can	17	*03:28
Leo	19	*14:52

1978

Sag	22	*11:30
Cap	24	*11:41
Aqu	26	*12:10
Pis	28	*14:37
Ari	30	*19:52
Tau	2	*03:50
Gem	4	*13:53
Can	7	*01:30
Leo	9	*14:07
Vir	12	*02:34
Lib	14	*12:54
Sco	16	*19:27
Sag	18	*21:59
Cap	20	*21:51

1979

Ari	21	*07:30
Tau	23	*11:20
Gem	25	*16:28
Can	27	*23:51
Leo	30	*10:08
Vir	1	*22:40
Lib	4	*11:10
Sco	6	*21:03
Sag	9	*03:13
Cap	11	*06:23
Aqu	13	*08:06
Pis	15	*09:56
Ari	17	*12:52
Tau	19	*17:18
Gem	21	*23:23

♊ Gemini – Finding Your Moon Sign ☽

1980		
Vir	21	*17:32
Lib	24	*06:10
Sco	26	*18:36
Sag	29	*05:04
Cap	31	*13:13
Aqu	2	*19:29
Pis	5	*00:09
Ari	7	*03:22
Tau	9	*05:29
Gem	11	*07:22
Can	13	*10:30
Leo	15	*16:22
Vir	18	*01:47
Lib	20	*13:55

1981		
Cap	21	*16:19
Aqu	24	*02:59
Pis	26	*11:04
Ari	28	*15:42
Tau	30	*17:10
Gem	1	*16:48
Can	3	*16:38
Leo	5	*18:42
Vir	8	*00:26
Lib	10	*09:55
Sco	12	*21:54
Sag	15	*10:31
Cap	17	*22:20
Aqu	20	*08:35

1982		
Gem	23	*01:54
Can	25	*01:38
Leo	27	*02:27
Vir	29	*05:43
Lib	31	*12:03
Sco	2	*21:12
Sag	5	*08:31
Cap	7	*21:11
Aqu	10	*10:07
Pis	12	*21:43
Ari	15	*06:19
Tau	17	*11:05
Gem	19	*12:33
Can	21	*12:12

1983		
Lib	21	*21:11
Sco	24	*02:17
Sag	26	*09:27
Cap	28	*19:06
Aqu	31	*06:59
Pis	2	*19:41
Ari	5	*06:58
Tau	7	*15:03
Gem	9	*19:36
Can	11	*21:31
Leo	13	*22:21
Vir	15	*23:38
Lib	18	*02:37
Sco	20	*07:59

1984		
Pis	22	*14:08
Ari	25	*02:39
Tau	27	*14:12
Gem	29	*23:21
Can	1	*05:53
Leo	3	*10:18
Vir	5	*13:26
Lib	7	*16:03
Sco	9	*18:48
Sag	11	*22:26
Cap	14	*03:48
Aqu	16	*11:41
Pis	18	*22:18
Ari	21	*10:40

♊ Gemini – Finding Your Moon Sign ☽

1985		
Can	22	*11:03
Leo	24	*19:53
Vir	27	*02:05
Lib	29	*05:40
Sco	31	*07:07
Sag	2	*07:33
Cap	4	*08:34
Aqu	6	*11:53
Pis	8	*18:46
Ari	11	*05:24
Tau	13	*18:11
Gem	16	*06:45
Can	18	*17:21
Leo	21	*01:31

1986		
Sag	23	*16:56
Cap	25	*16:15
Aqu	27	*17:00
Pis	29	*20:55
Ari	1	*04:43
Tau	3	*15:45
Gem	6	*04:26
Can	8	*17:15
Leo	11	*05:11
Vir	13	*15:17
Lib	15	*22:36
Sco	18	*02:35
Sag	20	*03:35

1987		
Ari	22	*11:23
Tau	24	*18:39
Gem	27	*03:55
Can	29	*14:59
Leo	1	*03:25
Vir	3	*15:55
Lib	6	*02:23
Sco	8	*09:05
Sag	10	*11:51
Cap	12	*12:04
Aqu	14	*11:45
Pis	16	*12:55
Ari	18	*16:56
Tau	21	*00:09

1988		
Vir	23	*11:12
Lib	25	*23:48
Sco	28	*10:05
Sag	30	*16:56
Cap	1	*20:58
Aqu	3	*23:33
Pis	6	*02:00
Ari	8	*05:03
Tau	10	*09:02
Gem	12	*14:14
Can	14	*21:19
Leo	17	*06:57
Vir	19	*19:03

1989		
Cap	23	*03:53
Aqu	25	*11:00
Pis	27	*16:12
Ari	29	*19:25
Tau	31	*20:59
Gem	2	*22:02
Can	5	*00:18
Leo	7	*05:28
Vir	9	*14:30
Lib	12	*02:31
Sco	14	*15:10
Sag	17	*02:11
Cap	19	*10:40
Aqu	21	*16:56

♊ Gemini – Finding Your Moon Sign ☽

1990		
Tau	22	*07:41
Gem	24	*06:59
Can	26	*06:33
Leo	28	*08:30
Vir	30	*14:08
Lib	1	*23:31
Sco	4	*11:21
Sag	6	*23:59
Cap	9	*12:11
Aqu	11	*23:08
Pis	14	*07:59
Ari	16	*13:53
Tau	18	*16:42
Gem	20	*17:14

1991		
Lib	23	*03:08
Sco	25	*11:41
Sag	27	*22:21
Cap	30	*10:40
Aqu	1	*23:41
Pis	4	*11:35
Ari	6	*20:24
Tau	9	*01:11
Gem	11	*02:35
Can	13	*02:16
Leo	15	*02:11
Vir	17	*04:03
Lib	19	*09:02
Sco	21	*17:18

1992		
Pis	24	*08:24
Ari	26	*19:51
Tau	29	*04:15
Gem	31	*09:18
Can	2	*11:57
Leo	4	*13:34
Vir	6	*15:28
Lib	8	*18:33
Sco	10	*23:27
Sag	13	*06:28
Cap	15	*15:50
Aqu	18	*03:19
Pis	20	*15:59

1993		
Can	23	*20:37
Leo	26	*02:02
Vir	28	*05:46
Lib	30	*08:17
Sco	1	*10:22
Sag	3	*13:01
Cap	5	*17:26
Aqu	8	*00:40
Pis	10	*10:57
Ari	12	*23:13
Tau	15	*11:18
Gem	17	*21:10
Can	20	*04:04

1994		
Sco	22	*21:50
Sag	24	*21:43
Cap	26	*22:17
Aqu	29	*01:20
Pis	31	*08:03
Ari	2	*18:31
Tau	5	*07:13
Gem	7	*20:02
Can	10	*07:21
Leo	12	*16:28
Vir	14	*23:15
Lib	17	*03:47
Sco	19	*06:19
Sag	21	*07:32

♊ Gemini – Finding Your Moon Sign ☽

1995		
Pis	21	*11:41
Ari	23	*19:13
Tau	26	*05:46
Gem	28	*18:06
Can	31	*06:59
Leo	2	*19:16
Vir	5	*05:45
Lib	7	*13:11
Sco	9	*17:02
Sag	11	*17:49
Cap	13	*17:04
Aqu	15	*16:52
Pis	17	*19:13
Ari	20	*01:30

1996		
Leo	22	*16:27
Vir	25	*04:58
Lib	27	*15:32
Sco	29	*22:29
Sag	1	*01:41
Cap	3	*02:28
Aqu	5	*02:44
Pis	7	*04:19
Ari	9	*08:23
Tau	11	*15:11
Gem	14	*00:16
Can	16	*11:08
Leo	18	*23:21
Vir	21	*12:06

1997		
Sag	22	*06:50
Cap	24	*11:50
Aqu	26	*15:19
Pis	28	*18:17
Ari	30	*21:17
Tau	2	*00:39
Gem	4	*04:54
Can	6	*11:02
Leo	8	*19:58
Vir	11	*07:43
Lib	13	*20:34
Sco	16	*07:50
Sag	18	*15:38
Cap	20	*20:01

1998		
Tau	23	*12:05
Gem	25	*12:25
Can	27	*13:59
Leo	29	*18:38
Vir	1	*03:21
Lib	3	*15:17
Sco	6	*04:05
Sag	8	*15:33
Cap	11	*00:49
Aqu	13	*08:02
Pis	15	*13:30
Ari	17	*17:22
Tau	19	*19:47
Gem	21	*21:26

1999		
Vir	22	*04:15
Lib	24	*13:29
Sco	27	*01:05
Sag	29	*13:37
Cap	1	*02:05
Aqu	3	*13:36
Pis	5	*22:59
Ari	8	*05:07
Tau	10	*07:42
Gem	12	*07:48
Can	14	*07:14
Leo	16	*08:07
Vir	18	*12:13
Lib	20	*20:10

2000		
Aqu	23	*12:59
Pis	26	*01:06
Ari	28	*10:06
Tau	30	*15:00
Gem	1	*16:33
Can	3	*16:29
Leo	5	*16:45
Vir	7	*18:57
Lib	9	*23:59
Sco	12	*07:55
Sag	14	*18:17
Cap	17	*06:26
Aqu	19	*19:25

Ⅱ Gemini Mercury Signs ☿

DATES	TAURUS	GEMINI	CANCER
1930	21 May–14 Jun	14 Jun–22 Jun	
1931	21 May–11 Jun	11 Jun–22 Jun	
1932	21 May–2 Jun	2 Jun–16 Jun	16 Jun–21 Jun
1933	21 May–25 May	25 May–8 Jun	8 Jun–21 Jun
1934		21 May–1 Jun	1 Jun–22 Jun
1935	21 May–29 May	29 May–20 Jun	20 Jun–22 Jun
1936		21 May–21 Jun	
1937	21 May–13 Jun	13 Jun–22 Jun	
1938	21 May–13 Jun	13 Jun–22 Jun	
1939	21 May–31 May	31 May–13 Jun	13 Jun–22 Jun
1940	21 May	21 May–4 Jun	4 Jun–21 Jun
1941		21 May–29 May	29 May–21 Jun
1942		21 May–22 Jun	
1943	26 May–14 Jun	21 May–26 May	
		14 Jun–22 Jun	
1944	21 May–11 Jun	11 Jun–21 Jun	
1945	21 May–4 Jun	4 Jun–18 Jun	18 Jun–21 Jun
1946	21 May–27 May	27 May–10 Jun	10 Jun–22 Jun
1947		21 May–2 Jun	2 Jun–22 Jun
1948		21 May–28 May	28 May–21 Jun
1949		21 May–21 Jun	
1950	21 May–14 Jun	14 Jun–21 Jun	
1951	21 May–9 Jun	9 Jun–22 Jun	
1952	21 May–31 May	31 May–14 Jun	14 Jun–21 Jun
1953	21 May–23 May	23 May–6 Jun	6 Jun–21 Jun
1954		21 May–30 May	30 May–21 Jun
1955		21 May–22 Jun	
1956		21 May–21 Jun	
1957	21 May–12 Jun	12 Jun–21 Jun	

DATES	TAURUS	GEMINI	CANCER
1958	21 May–5 Jun	5 Jun–20 Jun	20 Jun–21 Jun
1959	21 May–28 May	28 May–11 Jun	11 Jun–22 Jun
1960		21 May–2 Jun	2 Jun–21 Jun
1961	21 May–28 May	28 May–21 Jun	
1962		21 May–21 Jun	
1963	21 May–14 Jun	14 Jun–22 Jun	
1964	21 May–9 Jun	9 Jun–21 Jun	
1965	21 May–2 Jun	2 Jun–16 Jun	16 Jun–21 Jun
1966	21 May–24 May	24 May–21 Jun	
1967		21 May–31 May	31 May–22 Jun
1968		21 May–29 May	29 May–13 Jun
		13 Jun–21 Jun	
1969		21 May–21 Jun	
1970	21 May–13 Jun	13 Jun–21 Jun	
1971	21 May–7 Jun	7 Jun–21 Jun	
1972	21 May–29 May	29 May–12 Jun	12 Jun–21 Jun
1973		21 May–4 Jun	4 Jun–21 Jun
1974		21 May–29 May	29 May–21 Jun
1975		21 May–22 Jun	
1976	20 May–13 Jun	13 Jun–21 Jun	
1977	21 May–10 Jun	10 Jun–21 Jun	
1978	21 May–3 Jun	3 Jun–17 Jun	17 Jun–21 Jun
1979	21 May–26 May	26 May–9 Jun	9 Jun–21 Jun
1980		20 May–31 May	31 May–21 Jun
1981		21 May–28 May	28 May–21 Jun
1982		21 May–21 Jun	
1983	21 May–14 Jun	14 Jun–21 Jun	
1984	20 May–7 Jun	7 Jun–21 Jun	
1985	21 May–30 May	30 May–13 Jun	13 Jun–21 Jun
1986	21 May–22 May	22 May–5 Jun	5 Jun–21 Jun
1987		21 May–30 May	30 May–21 Jun
1988		20 May–21 Jun	

DATES	TAURUS	GEMINI	CANCER
1989		21 May–28 May	28 May–12 Jun
		12 Jun–21 Jun	
1990	21 May–12 Jun	12 Jun–21 Jun	
1991	21 May–5 Jun	5 Jun–19 Jun	19 Jun–21 Jun
1992	20 May–26 May	26 May–9 Jun	9 Jun–21 Jun
1993		21 May–2 Jun	2 Jun–21 Jun
1994		21 May–13 Jun	13 Jun–21 Jun
1995		21 May–21 Jun	
1996	21 May–13 Jun	13 Jun–21 Jun	
1997	20 May–8 Jun	8 Jun–21 Jun	
1998	21 May–1 Jun	1 Jun–15 Jun	15 Jun–21 Jun
1999	21 May–23 May	23 May–7 Jun	7 Jun–21 Jun
2000	20 May–30 May	30 May–21 Jun	

Ⅱ Gemini Venus Signs ♀

YEAR	ARIES	TAURUS	GEMINI	CANCER	LEO
1930			21 May–25 May	25 May–19 Jun	19 Jun–21 Jun
1931	21 May	21 May–14 Jun	14 Jun–22 Jun		
1932		21 May–2Jun	2 Jun–16 Jun	16 Jun–21 Jun	
1933			21 May–8 Jun	8 Jun–21 Jun	
1934	21 May–2 Jun	2 Jun–22 Jun			7 Jun–22 Jun
1935			29 May–21 Jun	21 May–7 Jun	
1936		21 May–29 May			
1937	21 May–4 Jun	4 Jun–22 Jun			18 Jun–22 Jun
1938		21 May–14 Jun	21 May–24 May	24 May–18 Jun	
1939			14 Jun–22 Jun	21 May–21 Jun	
1940				7 Jun–21 Jun	
1941			21 May–7 Jun		
1942	21 May–2 Jun	2 Jun–22 Jun			
1943			21 May–7 Jun	7 Jun–22 Jun	
1944		21 May–29 May	29 May–21 Jun		
1945	21 May–4 Jun	4 Jun–21 Jun			
1946	21 May–24 May	24 May–18 Jun	18 Jun–22 Jun		
1947		21 May–13 Jun	13 Jun – 22 Jun		
1948				21 May–21 Jun	
1949			21 May–7 Jun	7 Jun–21 Jun	
1950	21 May–1 Jun	1 Jun–21 Jun			

YEAR	ARIES	TAURUS	GEMINI	CANCER	LEO
1951		21 May–28 May; 5 Jun–21 Jun	28 May–21 Jun	21 May–7 Jun	7 Jun–22 Jun
1952	21 May–5 Jun				
1953		21 May–13 Jun	21 May–23 May; 13 Jun–21 Jun	23 May–17 Jun	17 Jun–22 Jun
1954					
1955					
1956				21 May–21 Jun	
1957				6 Jun–21 Jun	
1958	21 May–1 Jun	1 Jun–21 Jun	21 May–6 Jun	21 May–6 Jun	6 Jun–22 Jun
1959				21 Jun	
1960	21 May–5 Jun	21 May–28 May; 5 Jun–21 Jun	28 May–21 Jun		
1961				23 May–17 Jun	17 Jun–21 Jun
1962		21 May–12 Jun	21 May–23 May; 12 Jun–22 Jun		
1963				21 May–17 Jun	17 Jun–21 Jun
1964			21 May–6 Jun	6 Jun–21 Jun	
1965					
1966	21 May–31 May	31 May–21 Jun	27 May–21 Jun	21 May–6 Jun	6 Jun–22 Jun
1967				21 Jun	
1968	21 May–6 Jun	21 May–27 May; 6 Jun–21 Jun	21 May–22 May; 12 Jun–22 Jun		
1969				22 May–16 Jun	16 Jun–21 Jun
1970		21 May–12 Jun	21 May–5 Jun	22 Jun	
1971				20 May–11 Jun	
1972				5 Jun–21 Jun	11 Jun–21 Jun
1973					
1974	21 May–31 May	31 May–21 Jun		21 May–6 Jun	6 Jun–22 Jun
1975					

117

YEAR	ARIES	TAURUS	GEMINI	CANCER	LEO
1976		20 May–27 May	27 May–20 Jun	20 Jun–21 Jun	
1977	21 May–6 Jun	6 Jun–21 Jun			
1978			21 May–22 May	22 May–16 Jun	16 Jun–21 Jun
1979		21 May–11 Jun	11 Jun–21 Jun		
1980			5 Jun–21 Jun	20 May–5 Jun	
1981			21 May–5 Jun	5 Jun–21 Jun	
1982	21 May–30 May	30 May–21 Jun			
1983				21 May–6 Jun	6 Jun–21 Jun
1984		20 May–26 May	26 May–20 Jun	20 Jun–21 Jun	
1985	21 May–6 Jun	6 Jun–21 Jun			
1986			21 May	21 May–15 Jun	15 Jun–21 Jun
1987		21 May–11 Jun	11 Jun–21 Jun		
1988				20 May–27 May	27 May–21 Jun
1989			21 May–4 Jun	4 Jun–21 Jun	
1990	21 May–6 Jun	6 Jun–21 Jun			
1991				20 May–6 Jun	6 Jun–21 Jun
1992		21 May–26 May	26 May–19 Jun	19 Jun–21 Jun	
1993	21 May–6 Jun	6 Jun–21 Jun			
1994			21 May	21 May–15 Jun	15 Jun–21 Jun
1995		21 May–10 Jun	10 Jun–21 Jun		
1996			20 May–21 Jun		
1997			21 May–4 Jun	4 Jun–21 Jun	
1998	21 May–29 May	29 May–21 Jun			
1999				21 May–5 Jun	5 Jun–21 Jun
2000		20 May–25 May	25 May–18 Jun	18 Jun–21 Jun	

The Gemini Workbook

There are no right or wrong answers in this chapter. Its aim is to help you assess how you are doing with your life – in YOUR estimation – and to make the material of this book more personal and, I hope, more helpful for you.

1. The Gemini in You
Which of the following Gemini characteristics do you recognise in yourself?

versatile	cultured	curious
fun	witty	trend-spotting
stimulating	persuasive	inventive
sociable	charming	logical

2. In which situations do you find yourself acting like this?

_____

_____

3. When you are feeling vulnerable, you may show some of the less constructive Gemini traits. Do you recognise yourself in any of the following?

glib	inconsistent	two-faced
superficial	garrulous	amoral
irresponsible	nosy	slippery

What kind of situations trigger off this behaviour and what do you think might help you, in these situations, to respond more positively?

_____

_____

4. You and Your Roles
a) Where, if anywhere, in your life do you play the role of Go-between?

_____

_____

b) Whom, or what, do you link up?

_____

_____

5. Do you play any of the following roles – in the literal or broad senses – in any part of your life? If not, would you like to? What might be your first step towards doing so?

Broker   Messenger   Salesperson
Translator   Reporter/Commentator   Student

_____

_____

6. Sun Aspects
If any of the following planets aspects your Sun, add each of the keywords for that planet to complete the following sentences. Which phrases ring true for you?

I am _____

My father is _____

My job requires that I am _____

Saturn Words (Use only if your Sun is aspected by Saturn)

ambitious	controlling	judgmental	mature
serious	strict	traditional	bureaucratic
cautious	committed	hard-working	disciplined
depressive	responsible	status-seeking	limiting

Uranus Words (Use only if your Sun is aspected by Uranus)

freedom-loving	progressive	rebellious	shocking
scientific	cutting-edge	detached	contrary
friendly	disruptive	eccentric	humanitarian
innovative	nonconformist	unconventional	exciting

Neptune Words (Use only if your Sun is aspected by Neptune)

sensitive	idealistic	artistic	impressionable
disappointing	impractical	escapist	self-sacrificing
spiritual	unrealistic	dreamy	glamorous
dependent	deceptive	rescuing	blissful

Pluto Words (Use only if your Sun is aspected by Pluto)

powerful	single-minded	intense	extreme
secretive	rotten	passionate	mysterious
investigative	uncompromising	ruthless	wealthy
abusive	regenerative	associated with sex, birth or death	

a) If one or more negative words describe you or your job, how might you turn that quality into something more positive or satisfying?

_____

_____

7. The Moon and You

Below are brief lists of what the Moon needs, in the various elements, to feel secure and satisfied. First find your Moon element, then estimate how much of each of the following you are expressing and receiving in your life, especially at home and in your relationships, on a scale of 0 to 5 where 0 = none and 5 = plenty.

FIRE MOONS — Aries, Leo, Sagittarius

attention	action	drama
recognition	self-expression	spontaneity
enthusiasm	adventure	leadership

EARTH MOONS — Taurus, Virgo, Capricorn

stability	orderly routine	sensual pleasures
material security	a sense of rootedness	control over your home life
regular body care	practical achievements	pleasurable practical tasks

AIR MOONS — Gemini, Libra, Aquarius

mental rapport	stimulating ideas	emotional space
friendship	social justice	interesting conversations
fairness	socialising	freedom to circulate

WATER MOONS — Cancer, Scorpio, Pisces

intimacy	a sense of belonging	emotional rapport
emotional safety	respect for your feelings	time and space to retreat
acceptance	cherishing and being cherished	warmth and comfort

a) Do you feel your Moon is being 'fed' enough?

yes _____ no _____

b) How might you satisfy your Moon needs even better?

_____

_____

8. You and Your Mercury

As a Gemini, your Mercury can only be in Taurus, Gemini or Cancer. Below are some of the ways and situations in which Mercury in each of the elements might learn and communicate effectively. First find your Mercury sign, then circle the words you think apply to you.

Mercury in Fire (As a Gemini you can never have Mercury in a fire sign; the words are included here for completeness)

action	imagination	identifying with the subject matter
excitement	drama	playing with possibilities

Mercury in Earth (Taurus)

time-tested methods	useful facts	well-structured information
'how to' instructions	demonstrations	hands-on experience

Mercury in Air (Gemini)

facts arranged in categories	logic	demonstrable connections
rational arguments	theories	debate and sharing of ideas

Mercury in Water (Cancer)

pictures and images	charged atmospheres	feeling-linked information
intuitive understanding	emotional rapport	being shown personally

123

a) This game with Mercury can be done with a friend or on your own. Skim through a magazine until you find a picture that interests you. Then describe the picture – to your friend, or in writing or on tape. Notice what you emphasise and the kind of words you use. Now try to describe it using the language and emphasis of each of the other Mercury modes. How easy did you find that? Identifying the preferred Mercury style of others and using that style yourself can lead to improved communication all round.

9. Your Venus Values

Below are lists of qualities and situations that your Venus sign might enjoy. Assess on a scale of 0 to 5 how much your Venus desires and pleasures are met and expressed in your life. 0 = not at all, 5 = fully.

Venus in Aries

You will activate your Venus by taking part in anything that makes you feel potent, for example:

taking the initiative	competition	risk-taking
action dramas	taking the lead	tough challenges

Venus in Taurus

You will activate your Venus through whatever pleases the senses and enhances your sense of stability, for example:

financial security	beauty	gardening and nature
sensual pleasures	good food	body pampering

Venus in Gemini

You will activate your Venus through anything that stimulates your mind and uses a talent for making connections, for example:

playing go-between	flirting	talking and writing
passing on new ideas	witty use of words	trend-spotting

Venus in Cancer

You will activate your Venus through anything that makes you feel wise, intuitive, nurturing and nurtured, and at the centre of a 'family', for example:

a beautiful home	tenderness	sharing meals with loved ones
sharing feelings safely	home comforts	your family or country history

Venus in Leo

You will activate your Venus through anything that makes you feel special, unique, radiant and generous, for example:

extravagant gestures	luxury goods	prestigious activities
being central in a drama	acting nobly	being in love

a) How, and where, might you have more fun and pleasure by bringing more of what your Venus sign loves into your life?

_____

_____

b) Make a note here of the kind of gifts your Venus sign would love to receive. Then go on and spoil yourself . . .

_____

_____

Resources

Finding an Astrologer
I'm often asked what is the best way to find a reputable astrologer. Personal recommendation by someone whose judgement you trust is by far the best way. Ideally, the astrologer should also be endorsed by a reputable organisation whose members adhere to a strict code of ethics, which guarantees confidentiality and professional conduct.

Contact Addresses
Association of Professional Astrologers International
www.professionalastrologers.org
  APAI members adhere to a strict code of professional ethics.

Astrological Association of Great Britain
www.astrologicalassociation.co.uk
  The main body for astrology in the UK, with links to similar organisations throughout the world.

Faculty of Astrological Studies
www.astrology.org.uk
  The teaching body internationally recognised for excellence in astrological education at all levels.

Jane Ridder-Patrick
www.janeridderpatrick.com

Your Gemini Friends

You can keep a record of Geminis you know here, with the page numbers of where to find their descriptions handy for future reference.

Name _____ Date of Birth _____

Aspects★	None	Saturn	Uranus	Neptune	Pluto

Moon Sign _____ p _____

Mercury Sign _____ p _____

Venus Sign _____ p _____

Name _____ Date of Birth _____

Aspects★	None	Saturn	Uranus	Neptune	Pluto

Moon Sign _____ p _____

Mercury Sign _____ p _____

Venus Sign _____ p _____

Name _____ Date of Birth _____

Aspects★	None	Saturn	Uranus	Neptune	Pluto

Moon Sign _____ p _____

Mercury Sign _____ p _____

Venus Sign _____ p _____

Name _____ Date of Birth _____

Aspects★	None	Saturn	Uranus	Neptune	Pluto

Moon Sign _____ p _____

Mercury Sign _____ p _____

Venus Sign _____ p _____

★ Circle where applicable

Sign Summaries

SIGN	GLYPH	APPROX DATES	SYMBOL	ROLE	ELEMENT	QUALITY	PLANET	GLYPH	KEYWORD
1. Aries	♈	21/3 – 19/4	Ram	Hero	Fire	Cardinal	Mars	♂	Assertiveness
2. Taurus	♉	20/4 – 20/5	Bull	Steward	Earth	Fixed	Venus	♀	Stability
3. Gemini	♊	21/5 – 21/6	Twins	Go-Between	Air	Mutable	Mercury	☿	Communication
4. Cancer	♋	22/6 – 22/7	Crab	Caretaker	Water	Cardinal	Moon	☽	Nurture
5. Leo	♌	23/7 – 22/8	Lion	Performer	Fire	Fixed	Sun	☉	Glory
6. Virgo	♍	23/8 – 22/9	Maiden	Craftworker	Earth	Mutable	Mercury	☿	Skill
7. Libra	♎	23/9 – 22/10	Scales	Architect	Air	Cardinal	Venus	♀	Balance
8. Scorpio	♏	23/10 – 23/11	Scorpion	Survivor	Water	Fixed	Pluto	♇	Transformation
9. Sagittarius	♐	22/11 – 21/12	Archer	Adventurer	Fire	Mutable	Jupiter	♃	Wisdom
10. Capricorn	♑	22/12 – 19/1	Goat	Manager	Earth	Cardinal	Saturn	♄	Responsibility
11. Aquarius	♒	20/1 – 19/2	Waterbearer	Scientist	Air	Fixed	Uranus	♅	Progress
12. Pisces	♓	20/2 – 20/3	Fishes	Dreamer	Water	Mutable	Neptune	♆	Universality